GREAT CAREERS IN THE SPORTS INDUSTRY™

DREAM JOBS

IN SPORTS MANAGEMENT AND ADMINISTRATION

JERI FREEDMAN

ROSEN
PUBLISHING®

New York

Published in 2013 by The Rosen Publishing Group, Inc.
29 East 21st Street, New York, NY 10010

Copyright © 2013 by The Rosen Publishing Group, Inc.

First Edition

Library of Congress Cataloging-in-Publication Data

Freedman, Jeri.
Dream jobs in sports management and administration/
Jeri Freedman.—1st ed.
    p. cm.—(Great careers in the sports industry)
Includes bibliographical references and index.
ISBN 978-1-4488-6901-5 (library binding)
1. Sports—Management—Vocational guidance—
Juvenile literature. 2. Sports administration—
Vocational guidance—Juvenile literature. I. Title.
GV713.F745 2013
796.06'9—dc23
                                                    2011039476

Manufactured in the United States of America

CPSIA Compliance Information: Batch #S12YA: For further information, contact Rosen
Publishing, New York, New York, at 1-800-237-9932.

CONTENTS

Introduction ————————————————————— 4

CHAPTER 1 **What Is Sports Management?** ————— 6

CHAPTER 2 **Preparing for a Sports Management Career** 21

CHAPTER 3 **Education for Sports Management** ———— 32

CHAPTER 4 **College Sports Management and Administration** ————————————————— 39

CHAPTER 5 **Professional Sports Careers** ——————— 51

CHAPTER 6 **Managing a Sports Facility** —————————— 60

CHAPTER 7 **Managing a Sports Organization** ————— 66

CHAPTER 8 **Nonsports Professionals in Sports** ———— 71

CHAPTER 9 **Managing Sports Tourism and Fitness** —— 78

CHAPTER 10 **Managing Sporting Special Events** ——— 85

College and University Programs in Sports Management and Administration ———— 98

A Career in Sports Management and Administration at a Glance ———————————————— 110

Bureau of Labor Statistics Information —————— 114

Glossary ————————————————————— 118

For More Information ———————————————— 121

For Further Reading ———————————————— 127

Bibliography ——————————————————— 130

Index —————————————————————————— 132

New York Giants senior vice president and general manager Jerry Reese (*left*) and head coach Tom Coughlin observe players at a National Football League (NFL) camp. Reese had positions as assistant coach at the University of Tennessee and scout for the Giants before becoming a general manager.

Many people dream of a job in sports. Most often they see themselves drafted for a major league sports team. However, only a few people achieve that goal, and those who do frequently have short careers as players. For those who love sports, there are other ways to have a career in the field of sports that allow them to earn a good living while working in an area that interests and excites them. There are a vast number of sports management jobs at the professional, college, and high school levels. Sports management and administration jobs enable people to work with athletes, sports teams, and sporting events up close, and they provide the satisfaction of being directly involved in the success of a sports team or event. At the same time, they often provide excellent salaries and benefits.

Sports management and administration is the area of sports involved in performing the activities necessary for running a team, sports facility, or event. Some of these jobs are directly involved with players; others involve business or media functions. People in some of these positions work with the public; others work behind the scenes.

Most people are unfamiliar with the range of jobs necessary to run a team, sports facility, or event. This book provides a look at the different types of jobs available. It discusses the academic and practical preparation necessary to obtain a job in sports management and administration and then explains what to expect in the specific types of jobs.

Chapter 1

WHAT IS SPORTS MANAGEMENT?

What exactly is "sports management and adminis-tration"? When most people think of sports, they think of fun, exciting, and challenging physical activi-ties. The field of sports is also a business, though. Like any business, sports must have people who organize, run, and maintain sports teams, facilities, and events. At the top level of management, often called the executive level, are the general managers of teams and facilities and the producers of sporting events. However, no one person can manage a major undertaking by him- or her-self. Many managers and administrators are necessary. Managers are responsible for planning and overseeing a particular area or department. They often supervise other employees. Administrators are often staff-level employ-ees who perform functions necessary to run the team, facility, or event. For example, the manager or director of media relations would be responsible for planning and control of the department that deals with the press and broadcast media. The broadcast coordinator would be an administrative employee responsible for making the arrangements for the TV crew that broadcasts the game. The coordinator would report to a manager. Most managers start out in administrative positions and move up through the ranks until they reach the level of manager. They may be promoted at one company or may change jobs to take a higher-level job in another venue. Those who run academic programs are also sometimes referred to as administrators rather than managers, but their job functions are similar.

For many people interested in sports, sports administration or management can provide a dream job. Philadelphia Eagles general manager Howie Roseman is one such person. According to the Philadelphia Eagles Web site, after serving two years as vice president of player personnel, Roseman was named the general manager of the team on January 29, 2010. At thirty-six years old, he became the youngest general manager in the National Football League.

In his current position, Roseman works closely with head coach Andy Reid in all aspects of the player personnel department. As general manager, he "manages the college and pro scouting staffs, organizes draft meetings and the draft board, scouts the top college players around the country and assists in formulating the roster throughout the year."

Roseman said being a general manager had been his dream since he was a child. "I'd be 9 or 10 [years old], people would ask what I was to do. I'd say, I'm going to be the general manager of a National Football League team. They used to laugh."

Roseman applied for job after job in the front office of NFL teams until he finally landed one as a salary cap/staff counsel with the Eagles in 2000. He eventually worked his way up to his dream job.

Some sports management jobs involve working directly with players—for example, negotiating contracts

Howie Roseman (*right*) is interviewed after achieving his dream job by becoming general manager of the Philadelphia Eagles in January 2010.

or overseeing player services necessary to keep a team running. Some sports management jobs have creative aspects such as public relations and promotion. Some are technical, and others involve specialized skills such as financial management. Some managerial and administrative jobs, such as communications positions, involve a great deal of contact with the public. Other positions, such as business management or information technology management, involve tasks and responsibilities similar to those found in non-sports-related companies. It is much cooler, however, to have one's office in a sporting facility or to be part of a major team's organization than to work in many other types of business environments. In addition, many sports management and administrative positions, such as those at high schools and colleges, provide one with the satisfaction of helping young people develop and succeed.

Because of the wide range of jobs, facilities, and sports, there is likely to be something to suit anyone's temperament, skills, and personality. Therefore, sports management is an excellent choice for an interesting career in an exciting industry. There is a lot more to the sports industry, though, than major league teams.

THE SPORTS INDUSTRY

The sports industry can be divided into segments, or various areas of activity. The most obvious aspect of sports

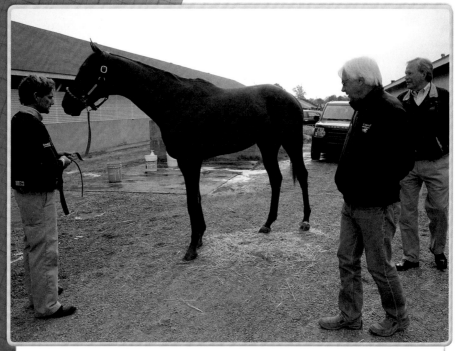

A racing manager (*far right*) surveys a horse after morning workouts in preparation for the running of the Kentucky Derby. The welfare of animals as well as athletes is an important responsibility for some sports managers.

is professional league sports such as baseball, basketball, hockey, football, and soccer. Even so, professional sports extend far beyond these team sports. Sports include a wide range of less well-known, or at least less frequently televised, team sports, as well as a wide variety of individual sports, including skiing, skating, golf, tennis, swimming, track and field, gymnastics, diving, rodeos, and professional bull riding, among others. For sports that involve animals, such as horse racing and bull riding, managers not only deal with the human athletes but oversee the acquisition, housing, and care of the animals as well.

MANAGING EXTREME SPORTS

A new type of sport has emerged in the past couple of decades—extreme sports. Extreme sports require great physical prowess and risk. They appeal to young people who find the risk and challenge exciting. Such sports include skateboarding, snowboarding, and aerial skiing, among others. Because of their enthusiastic following, more and more major competitions involving extreme sports are being produced. Athletes who participate in extreme sports must overcome not only their opponents but also environmental obstacles.

Some of the activities involved in organizing an extreme sporting event are similar to those of a traditional competition. For example, management must arrange for a suitable physical venue. However, the location of an extreme sporting event may be in a remote or inhospitable environment, such as mountains or rapids, which makes planning more difficult. Managers must create a schedule of events and heats, arrange for competitors to participate, arrange housing for the competitors, and provide viewing areas for the fans. They must oversee the physical layout of tracks and courses, and hire and supervise the courses' designers. They must have tickets printed and arrange for them to be sold directly and through various ticket outlets, such as Ticketmaster. The business or finance manager must keep an accounting of revenue and expenditures, and the security manager must ensure that personnel and systems are in place to keep viewers and participants safe. Information technology facilities must be provided for judging and timing events and

(continued on next page)

(continued from previous page)

for broadcasters. The public relations, marketing, or communications manager must arrange publicity for the event to attract fans. Medals and awards must be procured and award ceremonies organized.

In addition to these activities, however, managing extreme sports means maintaining physical facilities in unpredictable conditions, dealing with factors such as snow, ice, and wind, which may affect accessibility and the safety of competitors and fans. Those involved in managing extreme sporting events must also be prepared for a higher than usual number of accidents and injuries, including transporting those with serious injuries from a remote site to medical facilities. Because many extreme sporting events are broadcast on television, arranging suitable facilities for broadcasters is also a major concern.

Sports take place on an international as well as national level. Thus, one advantage of sports managerial and administrative jobs may be the chance to travel. Nevertheless, managing sports on an international level has unique challenges because one must deal with different cultures, laws, and languages.

Most sports require special facilities. These may be permanent, such as the Superdome in New Orleans, or temporary, such as the arenas built for Olympic events. Managers and administrators are needed to oversee the scheduling, maintenance, security, and information technology areas of these facilities, as well as the publicity and the vendors who supply food to patrons and supplies to sports teams.

Special events, such as the Olympics, are produced under the direction of either an individual hired to put the event together or an agency hired for this purpose. Sports management or administration of special events may be a temporary job, if the event occurs annually or less frequently. Working on such major events may be exciting and an excellent source of experience and contacts for future work. A job at an agency that regularly produces sporting events may provide more security, while also giving you the opportunity to work on a variety of different sporting events. Working for a sports organization can provide the satisfaction of helping to promote a sport you love.

Most sports have organizations devoted to promoting the sport and overseeing the competitions. Examples of such organizations are the Professional Golfers' Association (PGA) and the National Collegiate Athletic Association (NCAA). These organizations all require managers to run the organization and organize and promote the events.

Sports management jobs in all these areas will be described later in this book. Because of the wide range of areas in sports management, you should give some thought to what aspects of sports as well as what types of sports would interest you most. First, however, you should consider the nature of sports management and administration. Here is what Lee Igel, assistant professor at New York University's Tisch Center for Hospitality, Tourism & Sports Management, said about a sports management career, in an article by Matthew Lawyue: "'This is not *SportsCenter*; this is much more *Outside the Lines*,' Igel said, referring to two popular TV shows. 'It's very much about a series of conversations about management first and how it applies to the business of sports and how it fits into society.'"

PROFESSIONAL, SEMIPROFESSIONAL, AND ACADEMIC OPPORTUNITIES

Sports management opportunities are available at various levels, including high school and youth sports, college sports, semiprofessional sports, and professional sports. This chapter explores the nature of sports management and administration in these areas. Naturally, competition for positions increases as the level of professionalism rises. The fiercest competition will be for positions in professional sports teams in major markets.

HIGH SCHOOL AND YOUTH ATHLETICS

Although high school and youth sports take place at the local level, they are often overseen by local, state, and national organizations. These organizations arrange interstate and local competitions, promote participation in high school and youth sports, develop standards for eligibility, and run training programs for coaches and administrators of high school and youth sports. High school and youth teams require local managers and administrators who organize the teams and prepare them for competition. Some managerial and administrative positions in high school and youth sports include athletics director for high school sports, league manager for a youth league, team manager or coach, and trainer.

High school athletics directors fill a variety of roles. Here, the athletics director fills in as coach of the high school's girl's volleyball team, helping young athletes develop their skills.

One of the important jobs of those managing high school and youth teams is to participate in the state and national associations by serving on committees that develop the rules for eligibility, prepare the seasonal schedules, and decide on the rules of participation. In addition, the state and national associations require their own managers and administrators who create and distribute information about competitions, develop and run training programs, and coordinate member activities. Working with young athletes can be a highly fulfilling job, giving one the opportunity to develop talented young athletes into successful professionals.

COLLEGE SPORTS

College sports are second only to professional sports in generating public interest. Millions of people avidly follow the exploits of college football, basketball, hockey, track and field, and other sports. Today, a successful career in sports at the college level can provide an athlete with an entree to professional sports that means millions of dollars in pay and endorsement revenue. A successful team can also bring a college a great deal of broadcasting revenue, draw national attention to the college, and attract students. Therefore, team managers and coaches can have a very lucrative as well as exciting and fulfilling career at the college level. However, it can also be a high-pressure career, where there is a constant need to win.

The major organization overseeing college sports in the United States is the National Collegiate Athletic Association (NCAA). In Canada, the major organization governing college sports is Canadian Interuniversity Sport (CIS). Member colleges in the NCAA are divided into three divisions according to the size of the school. At Levels II and III, coaches may be part-time or cover more than one sport. Colleges in the top level, Level I, may have athletics department budgets of tens of millions of dollars. Level I sports departments are generally headed by an athletics director and have full-time coaches for major sports. Below the athletics director in the college athletic organization are various managers and administrators. Areas requiring managers and administrators include business management, ticket sales, athletic program administration, media relations, fundraising, marketing, facilities, and events coordination, among others. As in other areas of athletics, the professional organizations that oversee sports, such as the NCAA, also require managers and coordinators.

SEMIPROFESSIONAL SPORTS

Semiprofessional athletes are paid to play in a sport. However, most of them are part-time athletes because the amount they are paid is usually insufficient to provide their sole support. Therefore, they maintain a regular

Each One Teach One (EOTO) is a nonprofit basketball program designed to give high school players national exposure by giving them the chance to play Amateur Athletic Union basketball so that they might obtain scholarships to college.

career separate from their sports activity, and this other job provides most of their income. There are a number of semiprofessional sports leagues in the United States. These leagues are similar to minor league ball teams maintained by major league teams. There are formal organizations that assist in the promotion and running of semipro events. An example of such an organization is the Amateur Athletic Union (AAU). Semiprofessional sports sponsored by the AAU include baseball, basketball, football, gymnastics, martial arts, hockey, swimming, volleyball, wrestling, weightlifting, tennis, soccer, and lacrosse, among others. Olympic athletes who do not play on professional or semipro sports teams may also be considered semiprofessional athletes. Although they do not receive a salary to participate in their sport, they often receive money in the form of endorsements, which are agreements to promote the products of sporting goods and clothing manufacturers by wearing the company's logo or performing in TV commercials.

Semiprofessional teams require managers and administrators who help run the team and make the necessary arrangements for their games. As with players, these positions may be part-time. In some cases, they may be volunteer or internship positions. In addition, semiprofessional athletes, like their professional counterparts, often have agents—personal representatives who manage an athlete's career, including arranging endorsements and sponsorships.

PROFESSIONAL SPORTS

The largest and most complex area of sports is professional sports. The realm of professional sports involves very large organizations that run teams, facilities, events, and national associations. Millions of dollars often ride on the decisions made by managers in professional sports, and people in managerial and administrative positions are responsible for ensuring the successful outcome of events at the national and international level. Many managerial and administrative positions in professional sports are similar to their counterparts in other businesses: finance manager or accountant, security manager, information technology manager, network administrator, public relations director, and the like. Other positions, such as general manager, ticket sales manager, and sports agent have duties that are unique to the sports industry.

As you might expect, salaries for managers and administrators in professional sports are among the highest in the industry. However, the jobs are also often the most stressful because of the vast amount of money and prestige involved in professional sports. A career in professional sports can allow one to work closely with well-known athletes and to be involved in running events viewed by vast numbers of people. Managers and administrators in professional sports also require good people skills because they must deal with highly paid and successful athletes who are used to being treated with great respect. Working in professional sports can be one of the most satisfying career paths for those interested in a particular sport. The competition for such jobs is great, however. Therefore, the better your practical and academic preparations are, the better your chances of landing such a job.

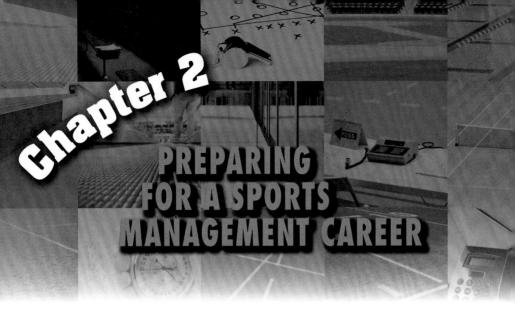

Chapter 2

PREPARING FOR A SPORTS MANAGEMENT CAREER

M any of the skills required to obtain a job as a manager or administrator in sports are similar to those required for managers and administrators in other fields. Others are unique to sports. Competition for jobs in the sports industry is keen. In addition to graduates with sports management degrees, individuals with degrees in communications, business, marketing, and finance often seek jobs in the field. For these reasons, academic knowledge is necessary but usually not sufficient to land a job in sports management and administration. Practical hands-on experience is usually necessary as well. This chapter describes both the academic and practical ways of preparing yourself.

The skills required for a sports management or administrative job vary according to the type of job you are interested in. Some general skills are important, however, regardless of the type of managerial or administrative job you are looking for.

SKILLS FOR SPORTS MANAGEMENT AND ADMINISTRATION

Any type of management job will require basic financial skills. Most managers must be able to perform tasks such as making out a departmental budget and keeping track of departmental expenditures to ensure that the amount spent doesn't exceed the budget. Most managerial and administrative jobs require a basic knowledge of statistics or the ability to use software that calculates

Managers in sports spend a significant amount of time on activities such as preparing budgets and reports, tracking projects, and performing other supervisory activities.

them. Managers and administrators need to know, for example, what percentage of tickets were sold by various ticket sales outlets, what type of advertising brings in the most fans per dollar spent, and the like. Another skill that is a necessity in any managerial or administrative position is the ability to communicate clearly, both verbally and in writing. Good writing skills are particularly important—a great deal of writing is involved in most jobs. Media or public relations jobs involve issuing written communications to the public, but all managerial positions involve a significant amount of writing, including reports, memos, lists of instructions, and business letters. You need a good understanding of English grammar to make sure that what you say is clearly understood. You also need to understand composition: how to write in an organized way so that you communicate clearly. A sound knowledge of grammar and syntax not only allows you to communicate clearly but also makes you appear and sound professional.

Many jobs in sports management and administration involve making presentations. Some positions require more extensive public speaking skills for addressing live audiences at events or speaking on radio or television. Therefore, good verbal communication skills are important for many jobs, including general management, media management and administration, and public relations management or administration.

However, all managers and administrators, even those who are rarely called on to speak in public, must have good listening skills and good verbal communication skills. A manager or administrator must often give instructions to employees, team members, vendors, and others involved in daily business activities. Good listening skills include paying close attention to what other people say and checking to make sure you have understood their point correctly. Good verbal communication skills include speaking clearly and concisely, verifying that others have understood you correctly, and allowing adequate time for others to respond to what you say. Good communication skills allow you and others to work more effectively and minimize misunderstandings. If you are interested in a career in general management or as a sports agent, you will also need to develop negotiating skills.

In today's technological world, it is very helpful to have computer skills. In management and administration, knowledge of business software is also helpful. Commonly used programs include spreadsheet software such as Microsoft Excel, presentation software such as Microsoft PowerPoint, and project management software. Project management software automates the tracking of different phases of a project and the resources in use.

LAYING THE GROUNDWORK

There are no courses in sports management and administration in high schools. However, you can take courses that will give you the skills you will need as a sports manager or administrator. Courses that help you hone your skills as a communicator, such as English composition and public speaking, will be of benefit. Math courses such as algebra and statistics will give you the basic skills to perform statistical analyses and mathematical calculations. If your school offers a course in using computers, it's a good idea to take it, especially if it covers basic word processing and business software such as spreadsheets. No matter what your job today is, if you are involved in management and administration, you inevitably find yourself using a computer and business software. For the same reason, it is very useful to take a typing course if your school offers one because you will probably spend a good deal of time working on a keyboard, especially in an entry-level job. Although it may not seem obvious, if you are interested in an area of sports such as training or coaching, courses in biology and physics will help you gain an understanding of the forces that affect the body in action.

In addition to studying, participating in a variety of sports will be beneficial because it will help you understand the different elements that are important in those sports.

If you do not qualify for the official high school team in a particular sport, it is still worthwhile to participate in intramural and community sports. Moreover, even if you are on a sports team or have a favorite sport, it is beneficial to participate in other types of sports during the off-season. If you do pursue a career in sports management and administration, you may find that you ultimately get a job in a sport other than your favorite one. You may even get a job that covers many sports, such as working at a facility where different sports are played in different seasons, or at an agency that manages various types of sporting events. Having knowledge—especially hands-on knowledge—of an array of sports can give you an advantage over other candidates when applying for a position.

ADVANTAGES OF A BROAD EDUCATION

The field of sports today is a global enterprise. Players for professional teams are recruited from throughout the world. Participants in conventional and extreme sporting events come from around the globe, and North American teams and individual athletes frequently travel to other countries to participate in international events. Thus, you must be able to work with people from a variety of backgrounds and in foreign settings. Courses in areas such as foreign languages and history can help you understand and communicate with people from other countries. Having this type of background can enhance your understanding of and tolerance for the cultures and beliefs of the athletes and other employees you come in contact with.

GAINING PRACTICAL EXPERIENCE

In today's competitive sports job market, it's beneficial to gain experience and exposure before starting to look for a job. Participating in the management and administration of school or community teams and sporting competitions is an excellent way to gain practical experience. Such participation will help you evaluate whether you enjoy the administrative side of sports. It will also provide you with experience you can include on your résumé when you apply for your first job. In addition, the adults you work with in these activities can provide you with valuable references when you are being considered for a job.

Working hands-on in the management and administrative side of sports gives you the opportunity to practice the skills that will be required on a larger scale in a professional position. It also provides the opportunity to learn professional behavior. One of the best ways to gain experience is to volunteer to work with sporting teams in your community. Most communities have Little League teams in a variety of sports. These teams require, on a small scale, much of the same management and administration as larger teams. Schedules must be drawn up for practices and games, materials must be prepared to

JOB OUTLOOK FOR SPORTS MANAGEMENT AND ADMINISTRATION JOBS

As reported by the U.S. Bureau of Labor Statistics (BLS) in the United States, sports are a $200 billion industry. According to the market research firm First Research, the U.S. professional sports industry contains 1,500 professional organizations. Plunkett Research estimates that NCAA sports produce $757 million in revenue. As claimed by the same source, there are 22,000 fitness and recreation companies and organizations operating about 30,000 fitness and recreation centers in the United States with revenues of $21 billion.

According to the BLS, job growth is expected to be faster than average between the present and 2018 in the athletics jobs that include coaches, sport instructors, sport officials, scouts, and related jobs. The rate of increase in jobs in these areas is expected to be 23 percent from 2008 to 2018. Still, the competition for positions in sports will be intense. In 2008, 52 percent of those in such positions were employed in public and private education facilities, and 13 percent worked in amusement and recreational facilities, including sports clubs and resorts, among other venues. The balance was employed in professional sports. Those who have state certification to teach are likely to be in highest demand in academic environments as coaches and athletic managers.

inform the public and parents of when and where games will take place, equipment needs to be organized, and players have to be supervised and trained.

Many cities and towns have semiprofessional teams in a variety of sports. These teams play against teams from other cities and towns. Contact the manager of the team in your town or city to see if there are volunteer positions available. Many towns and cities also sponsor summer sports programs for young people at parks or other recreational facilities. These programs rely heavily on volunteers, including teenagers, who are willing to organize and supervise sports for children. Contact your town or city hall recreation and parks department to see where volunteer opportunities exist for such programs.

Yet another volunteer program is run by ESPN Wide World of Sports Complex through its Web site (http://espnwwos.disney.go.com/about/volunteer). This program solicits sports enthusiasts to assist in running sporting events in their local communities. Sports fantasy and summer camps also provide opportunities to gain experience. Like conventional summer camps, sports camps can provide either volunteer or paid positions. Some professional sports teams have foundations that run sports summer camps or programs for children. The San Francisco Giants, for example, maintain the Giants Sports Foundation, which offers such camps for children and uses

This recent high school graduate is a volunteer who helps other teen athletes at his former school to improve their game. Volunteering is a great way to improve your skills and gain experience.

volunteers to help run its programs. Contact the professional teams in your area to see if they offer such programs. You can also type "sports foundation" and the name of your state into an Internet search engine to see some organizations that produce such programs and may use volunteers.

PARTICIPATING IN PROFESSIONAL ASSOCIATIONS

Another way to gain inside knowledge of sports management and administration is through participation in professional sports organizations. As mentioned previously, there are professional organizations at the local, state, and national level that oversee all types of sports at the high school, college, amateur, and professional level. Many such organizations offer student memberships or programs. Becoming a member of such an organization, reading its literature, and attending meetings can provide you with insight into the issues related to managing sports teams and events. Moreover, participating in professional organizations can allow you to develop contacts with professionals in sports, who may be able to provide you with advice on obtaining a job in the field when you are ready to do so.

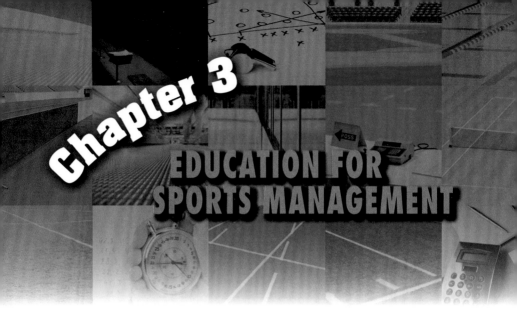

EDUCATION FOR
SPORTS MANAGEMENT

Chapter 3

Most sports management and administrative positions require a college degree. Although it is not necessary to major in sports management to obtain all positions in this field, if you wish to rise to the highest levels, either an undergraduate or graduate degree that focuses on sports management and administration is helpful in many cases. Many people in sports management and administration have degrees in other areas, however, including business, finance, law, and recreation and hospitality. This chapter examines the educational options for those interested in a career in sports management and administration.

COLLEGE PROGRAMS

A number of colleges offer four-year programs that lead to a bachelor's degree in sports management. In addition, it is possible to obtain a master's degree in sports management, a master of education degree in sports management, or a master of business administration (MBA) degree in sports management or sports business. It is also possible to obtain a two-year associate's (AA) degree that is suitable for obtaining entry-level jobs in the sports management field. A master's degree or MBA is beneficial to those who wish to pursue higher levels of management in sports. A master of education degree in sports management is useful for those interested in a career in high school or college athletics.

Taking high school courses in computer science, accounting and finance, project management, and other business areas helps prepare you for managerial responsibilities. Earning a college degree is crucial for obtaining many sports management positions.

It is also possible to obtain a Ph.D. in sports management, which is valuable for those who are interested in pursuing research in the field or participating in the highest level of sports management at colleges and universities. The coursework in the program you choose should focus on business and management skills, with the emphasis on how those skills are applied to sports as a business. The sports management degree programs at some colleges focus on the business side of sports, whereas others focus on the physical and training side of sports. So check out the actual courses in the program. Even if the program you choose does not require it, you should take courses in general business areas such as accounting and marketing so that you are adequately prepared to succeed in the business of sports.

Undergraduate programs tend to concentrate on equipping students with the basic knowledge they need to understand the sports industry. Examples of undergraduate courses include recreation and natural resources; commercial recreation, sport, and tourism; recreation and sport leadership; sport management fundamentals; program planning in sport and recreation; planning, design, and maintenance for sports and recreation; sport and recreation risk management; and outdoor adventure leadership, among others. It is common for undergraduate programs to require internships or practical courses, which allow students to practice what they learn in school in hands-on situations.

SPORTS MANAGEMENT INTERNSHIPS

Internships are unpaid jobs in organizations or companies. They give a person the chance to learn on-the-job skills and gain experience in a field. Those interested in sports management will benefit from participating in sports internships. Engaging in an internship provides you with job experience that shows potential employers that you can perform the tasks the job entails. Interns carry out basic tasks in the field, but more important, they have the chance to observe what professionals in the field do. Interns who perform well can get a reference that will help when they apply for their first paid job. Moreover, working with professionals in the field gives interns the chance to make valuable contacts that might be able to help them when they are looking for a job. Most colleges require internships as part of their sports management degree programs. Beyond that, many professional sports organizations offer internships. Web sites such as Internships.com list internships for college students in various areas of sports management and administration. The National Collegiate Athletic Association (NCAA) maintains a list of job postings for interns on its Web site as well, where member sports organizations post openings.

Graduate-level programs focus on the managerial and business aspects of sports. Examples of graduate-level courses include applied statistics; statistics and data processing for education; sport facilities management;

managerial communication; public and private finance; legal and political aspects of sports; sports finance; sports event management; contracts and negotiation; economics and revenue analysis in sports; sports marketing; sports promotion, licensing, and sponsorship; and sports and recreation service promotion, among others.

SPECIFIC VS. GENERAL EDUCATION FOR SPORTS MANAGEMENT

An alternative for those interested in a career in sports management is to combine another major with a minor in sports management. This approach allows a person to combine a primary interest in another academic area with an education in sports management and administration. This strategy is particularly beneficial for those interested in studying areas such as law, business, accounting, communications, media, public relations, or other professional areas as a primary discipline. If one has an interest in sports, combining such studies with additional coursework in sports management can equip one to pursue a career in such areas within the sports industry.

DEVELOPING A PROFESSIONAL OUTLOOK

Sports management is more than playing games—or watching them. It is necessary to develop a professional attitude and demeanor, and to understand sports as a

How you present yourself is always important in a career. Looking professional leads others to respect you and listen to what you say. Managers are expected to dress and speak well.

business. The sports industry is big business, and those in it must conduct themselves just like other business professionals. If you wish to obtain and succeed in a job in the field of sports management and administration, it is important that you conduct yourself professionally. Be prepared to dress appropriately. What is acceptable attire will vary depending on your exact job and whether you are working in an academic, recreational, or professional sports environment. Even so, many business-related jobs, especially those in which one deals with the public, require professionals to wear suits: neat dresses, skirts and blouses, or slacks for women and slacks, dress shirts, jackets, and ties for men. Even if your position allows you to dress casually, it is important to always wear neat, clean, proper clothing.

It is also important to conduct yourself professionally. On the job, show respect to your colleagues as well as your superiors. Show up on time and complete your assignments on time. This not only helps your own career but also relieves the burden on your colleagues, who are depending on you. If people respect you at work, they will not only be more likely to help advance your career but also more likely to help you when you have issues.

The time to start developing a professional attitude is while you are still in school and in your part-time or summer work. Take a respectful attitude toward others, and do your work on time and to the best of your ability. These habits will serve you well throughout your career.

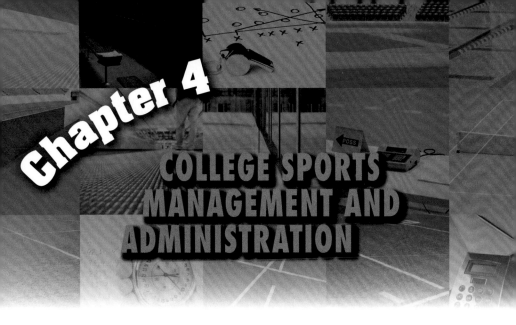

Chapter 4

COLLEGE SPORTS MANAGEMENT AND ADMINISTRATION

There are limited opportunities for professional managerial and administrative positions in high school sports. Most such duties fall to the coach or coaches of the school teams. High school coaching may be a dedicated position or a part-time position performed by a teacher with other teaching responsibilities.

College athletics are another matter entirely. Collegiate sports offer significant opportunities for those interested in a career in sports management and administration. Colleges come in a wide range of sizes, and the roles of athletics departments vary as well. In large colleges with prominent sports teams, the athletics program may have a multimillion-dollar budget and a large managerial team similar to that of a large company. All athletics programs require managers and administrators who must staff, direct, plan, and organize the program and perform financial management as well.

COLLEGE ATHLETIC PROGRAM SENIOR MANAGEMENT

At the top of the college athletics hierarchy is the athletics director. The athletics director is much like the chief executive officer of a large corporation. His or her job is to oversee the entire athletics organization. In this role the athletics director is responsible for financial management, media, legal compliance, safety and risk management, ticket sales, fund-raising, scheduling of games and events, and human resources.

A college athletics director meets with members of the press to discuss the college's response to a recent scandal. Damage control is one of the many responsibilities of athletics directors.

Today, college sports is big business, and most often colleges and universities need an athletics director with business experience and an advanced degree in business administration or sports management. The athletics director usually reports to the college president or a vice president.

A related position is assistant or associate athletics director. The person in this position helps the athletics director perform the functions already mentioned. He or she works with the middle-level managers to make sure that their departments are accomplishing their responsibilities so that the goals of the athletics program are met. Depending on the size of the college, an athletics director may have one or multiple assistant or associate directors. In a college with a large athletics program, the athletics director may have a number of assistant directors, each of whom is responsible for a specific area, such as media relations, compliance, ticket sales, marketing, facilities, events, fund-raising or development, accounting and finance, and equipment. The assistant or associate athletics director communicates with the coaches and department heads for the athletics director to see that activities are carried out according to the goals of the athletics department. The assistant or associate athletics director ensures that departments are performing appropriately on issues relating to human resources and compliance with governing rules and informs the athletics director of any issues that arise from the various departments so that they can be addressed.

Women's sports have been gaining in importance over the past couple of decades. Title IX, part of the 1972 amendment to the U.S. Civil Rights Act of 1964, mandates equal opportunity for women in education. One of its effects has been an increase in the number of women's sports teams. Many universities now have a dedicated women's athletics administrator or director who is in charge of the women's sports program. She is responsible for fund-raising, operations, marketing, and compliance for the women's sports. This is a high-level executive position and has become one of the most important positions for women in college sports management and administration.

Senior management positions at a college or university generally require a master's degree or Ph.D.

MANAGERIAL AND ADMINISTRATIVE POSITIONS IN COLLEGE ATHLETICS

Managerial and administrative positions involved in the business side of college athletics include the athletics development director, facilities manager, ticket manager, business or finance manager, and championship and special events manager. Each of the areas headed by a manager is staffed by administrative personnel, such as ticket agents, facilities personnel, accountants, customer service agents, sales personnel, and events staff.

The job of the athletics development manager is to obtain donations from alumni or other sources and to produce fund-raising events to raise money for the athletics department. The business or finance manager is responsible for keeping track of the expenditures and revenues and ensuring that the department stays on budget. He or she prepares reports on the financial state of the department for the athletics director and oversees all the financial aspects of running the athletics department. The ticket manager is responsible for overseeing the sale of tickets to the public and keeping track of money received for them. Those in business and financial positions will most likely have an undergraduate or graduate degree in business or finance.

College facilities also require managers. Facilities managers are responsible for the upkeep of the gym, playing field, swimming pool, sports arena, and other sports facilities. Major colleges and universities have extensive sports facilities, and the importance of this position has grown along with the significance of college sports. It is common for facilities managers to have a degree in engineering or architecture. The equipment manager must handle the purchasing and maintenance of sports equipment used by the college athletics program. He or she is

An assistant athletics director for event management and facilities gets ready for the start of a football game, ensuring that everything is prepared for the game to proceed smoothly.

responsible for keeping track of the inventory of equipment and making sure that purchasing and maintenance are performed within budget.

College sports are nothing without players. The recruiting manager or coordinator is responsible for evaluating potential athletes for the school's major sports teams, such as football and basketball. He or she must then persuade these athletes to attend the school. In this role, recruiters work with the recruiting staff, professors, college administrators, and coaches to determine if candidates are eligible for scholarships. Because recruiters spend a great deal of time speaking with teenagers, high school coaches, and parents, they must have very good people skills and be good communicators who can convince prospects that their school is the one to attend. In addition, they must have the skills to evaluate prospects' athletic ability. Those who obtain this position generally have a college degree and coaching experience, which enables them to evaluate athletic prowess.

No matter how great a college's teams are, what produces revenue is getting people to watch the games. That's where the ticket manager comes in. This is a very important position, especially at large schools, where revenue from ticket sales can be millions of dollars. The ticket manager's job is to stimulate ticket sales, track ticket revenues, and do the accounting for ticket sales. The ticket manager supervises employees involved in selling and accounting

THE MANAGER
AS A LEADER

Most descriptions of careers in sports management concentrate on the specific duties of the manager or administrator. One of the greatest influences on a person's ability to succeed in any managerial or administrative position, however, is his or her ability to perform as a leader. The fact of the matter is that all managers must deal with people—employees, fans, players, player representatives, and regulators. This is where being a leader counts. Leaders have qualities that make people want to follow them and achieve a goal, and abilities that allow them to manage people successfully.

Among the chief qualities a leader has are the following:

- *A vision of how things could be. People work harder when they feel they are working toward a specific end that is important.*

- *The drive and commitment to work hard toward achieving a goal. People work harder for a person they think is working hard.*

- *Good organizational skills. A leader can successfully organize people and resources to achieve a goal.*

- *Great written and verbal communication skills. A leader can communicate clearly what must be done and why. Most important, a leader can motivate and inspire others.*

for ticket sales. He or she develops incentives—special promotions—to increase ticket sales, such as group packages, corporate ticket sales, and season ticket sales. The ticket manager is also responsible for dealing with customer service problems that arise. This position generally requires a degree in accounting or business.

A special aspect of college athletics is the need to comply with the regulations of state, national, and international organizations regulating college sports. This is the role of the compliance manager. This person must stay up to date on regulations, communicate with representatives of organizations that oversee college sports, and monitor the college athletes and teams to make sure that they do not violate any regulations.

A position that has been growing in significance over the past couple of decades is student athletic services manager. The person in this role is responsible for ensuring that athletes' academic and personal well-being is maintained. He or she is responsible for seeing that student athletes are functioning satisfactorily in their academic coursework and that they have tutors if needed. College athletes undergo a great deal of stress and face many temptations. It is the student athletic services manager's responsibility to see that students receive counseling if necessary for any problems they have. Those in this position may have an education or counseling degree.

COMMUNICATIONS CAREERS

There are many managerial and administrative positions in sports that relate to media and communications at colleges. Some positions deal with students, some deal with the public, and others deal with the media. Among these positions are community relations manager, public relations manager, and media coordinator. The community relations manager is responsible for working with officials of the town or city in which the college or university is located to ensure that good relations are maintained between the town and college.

Here, an associate athletics director in charge of communications holds a press conference to provide members of the media with news about a college sports team.

The public relations manager is responsible for keeping the public informed about the athletic events and activities of the sports team at the school. He or she must write press releases and distribute them to the media to publicize upcoming events and the achievements of the athletes and teams. Public relations managers must also talk to members of the media in response to both positive and negative occurrences that relate to the athletes and athletic events at the college. The public relations manager may also be responsible for seeing that information about the athletes and events is shared over electronic media such as a blog or social media outlets like Twitter and Facebook.

College sports are often broadcast on television. The media coordinator is responsible for making arrangements for the broadcasting of college games and events. He or she may participate in arranging contracts for broadcasting games and coordinate the activities of broadcasters. Those involved in communications positions usually require a degree in an area such as communications or public relations. A graduate degree in either a communications area or sports management increases your chances of obtaining this type of position.

COLLEGE TEAM CONFERENCE CAREERS

Major college sports are divided into conferences, consisting of a number of teams from a specific region. Each of the conferences has a staff, which is responsible for overseeing the colleges in their conference. Managerial and administrative positions include enforcement and compliance, marketing, championship administration, public relations, officiating, and broadcasting. Those in these areas are responsible for providing services for all the teams in the conference. The responsibilities of those in marketing, public relations, and broadcasting are similar to their counterparts' in the colleges, except that they perform these functions for the conference as a whole. Enforcement and compliance involve ensuring that the member teams are following all the rules and that any violations are addressed. Officiating consists of recruiting, training, and scheduling officials for competitions, as well as making travel arrangements for them.

Chapter 5

PROFESSIONAL SPORTS CAREERS

The height of sports careers is professional sports. This is the biggest stage and provides the most dramatic events. When people think of professional sports, they often focus on major team sports: football, basketball, baseball, soccer, and hockey. Nonetheless, professional sports encompass any sports activity in which athletes are paid for their participation, including major and minor league sports teams and sports in which individual athletes support themselves through the revenues they earn in their sport. Examples of professional sports include skiing, racing, tennis, and golf, among others. Professional teams and organizations that put on sports tournaments make money by selling tickets and rights to broadcast games, as well as through licensed merchandise. Semipro teams and sports are similar to their professional counterparts but the managerial and administrative positions are generally part-time paid or volunteer positions.

PLAYER PERSONNEL

Professional team sports require managers and administrators in positions responsible for locating, evaluating, and assembling a team of players. Examples of such positions include the scouting manager and scouts, human resources manager and staff, and general manager.

The general manager is responsible for overseeing all aspects of player management. He or she is responsible for decisions regarding the scouting of players, signing players, negotiating contracts with players, and trading players. Some teams prefer individuals with an

Billy Beane (*second from left*), general manager of the Oakland Athletics major league baseball team, spends time with operations staff in the clubhouse prior to the start of a ballgame.

advanced degree in sports management or law for this position. Other teams have general managers with more practical experience in areas such as coaching and rely on assistant managers with degrees in sports management or law to take charge of contract negotiations. One unique aspect of professional team sports is that in many major leagues players belong to a union. Under a union arrangement players engage in collective bargaining. In this model, the team's management must reach an agreement on pay, benefits, and other issues with representatives of the players' union. The agreement they reach is formalized as a contract and applies to all players. Thus, general management must be experienced and skillful at negotiating, not just with players' representatives but with the union representatives as well.

The scouting manager and scouts are responsible for identifying likely prospects, evaluating them, and reporting with recommendations to the general manager. Scouting involves a great deal of travel to observe and evaluate candidates.

The human resources manager and staff are responsible for overseeing the hiring process for employees of the team and making sure that hiring and management practices conform to the laws governing these areas. For example, they make sure the team complies with laws mandating equal opportunity and protection against sexual harassment. They provide information and assistance

Scouts and coaches time players running sprints at an NFL combine event to assess athletes and advise general managers about possible acquisitions for their teams.

in areas relating to benefits such as insurance and retirement plans. They also work with managers to resolve any issues with employees.

Professional athletes are not like other employees in a business. They earn large salaries and are often in the public eye. Because they are often young, they may lack experience dealing with many issues arising from celebrity. Staff members in player education and relations are responsible for working with players on issues such as financial management, image management, and healthy habits like maintaining good nutrition and avoiding substance abuse. They also manage community appearances by players.

MENTORING

A mentor is an experienced person with expertise in a particular area who is willing to give a less experienced person guidance and support. Having a mentor can help you learn skills faster and avoid mistakes. A mentor can also give you advice when you run into problems. In a business setting, a more experienced professional will often take an interest in a younger, less experienced staff member if that person is talented and works hard. However, you can also approach a person whose expertise and knowledge you respect, and ask if he or she would be willing to act as your mentor. Explain why you chose that person and

(continued on next page)

West Side High School in Newark, New Jersey, and Seton Hall University's Stillman School of Business have formed a "Junior MBA" program to provide students with mentoring. Many colleges team up with high schools to offer students mentoring opportunities.

(continued from previous page)

what type of guidance you seek. If that person is too busy to help, he or she may be able to recommend someone who can.

If a person agrees to become your mentor, communicate with him or her regularly about the activities you are involved in and the issues you are dealing with. Usually, a mentor has behind-the-scenes knowledge of how things work in the organization and what has succeeded or failed in the past. Therefore, his or her input is valuable. You may not always agree with the advice your mentor gives; however, you should always treat him or her with respect. Give your mentor feedback about what worked and what didn't. Be sure to show that you appreciate the time your mentor is taking to help you succeed and express your thanks for his or her help.

STADIUM AND FACILITY POSITIONS IN PRO SPORTS

The stadium manager and staff are responsible for the upkeep of the physical building and playing area where the sport takes place. They are responsible for the maintenance and repair of the team's office and locker room as well as the actual stadium or playing field. Equipment and clubhouse personnel are responsible for the ordering, maintenance, and repair of equipment and uniforms. They are responsible for seeing that everything necessary for the team to play is packed and shipped. They also evaluate and order new equipment.

COMMUNICATIONS POSITIONS

The video support coordinator and staff are responsible for producing team videos and taping games. They purchase and use video production hardware and software. They are responsible for maintaining the satellite connection for broadcasting games and supervising the broadcasting. They also maintain the library of the team's videos.

Community and public relations managers and employees perform functions similar to those of their college athletics counterparts. They provide information on the team and its activities to the media and work with the community to maintain a mutually beneficial relationship with the citizens of the town or city where the team is located. The team may have its own advertising manager and personnel or use an advertising agency to create and place ads promoting the team's games and other activities.

BUSINESS POSITIONS IN PRO SPORTS

The ticket sales manager and staff are responsible for selling tickets to the public, monitoring tickets sales, and tracking the revenue from ticket sales. Professional sports teams have a special ticket sales area called corporate sales. Those in this area are responsible for selling blocks of tickets to companies, which then distribute them to their customers or employees. The staff members in this area also sell season tickets to corporations for the same purpose.

The financial manager works with the ticket manager to track revenues and expenses to establish the best mix of pricing and promotions to cover expenses and maximize profit.

As in other businesses, professional sports teams require financial managers and staff. These individuals are responsible for budgeting and keeping track of the team's revenue and expenses. They use computer software to manage the team's financial accounts and prepare financial reports. The financial manager may also be involved in managing funds for projects such as building new facilities or buying major equipment.

As in most large companies today, professional sports organizations require computer technology to function. The information technology (IT) manager and crew purchase, install, maintain, repair, and upgrade computer hardware and software. They also maintain the team's computer network and databases of information, and set up and maintain the team's Web site.

OBTAINING A JOB IN PRO SPORTS

Managerial and administrative positions in professional sports organizations usually require a college degree. For managerial positions, an advanced degree is desirable. A manager's degree may be in sports management, but in positions such as IT, communications, and finance, successful candidates will often have a degree in one of these areas. A bachelor's degree in a specific area such as communications, IT, or finance can also be combined with a master's degree in sports management, or vice versa.

There is great competition for jobs in pro sports because of the appeal of working in the sports field, the prestige of working for a professional sports organization, and the good pay and benefits. For the same reasons, turnover (employees leaving and being replaced) tends to be low. Academic preparation and practical experience as an intern are important to being competitive in the field. Most of those who obtain a job in professional sports start in an entry-level position in an area such as sales or customer service and work their way up to areas of greater responsibility.

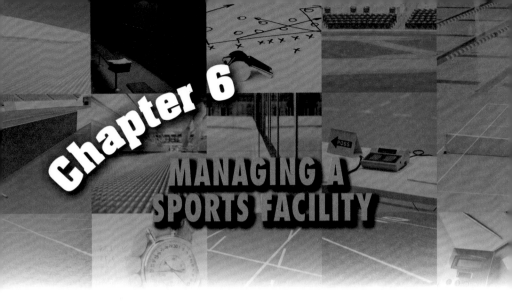

Chapter 6

MANAGING A SPORTS FACILITY

Sports take place in a variety of venues for public viewing. This chapter covers the types of positions involved in managing a range of sports facilities. The primary types of facilities used in sports are stadiums and arenas. Stadiums are large facilities either open to the air or domed. They are used by football, soccer, and baseball teams. Arenas are similar to stadiums, but they are smaller, indoor facilities. They are used by basketball and hockey teams, but also for a wide range of other sports, from volleyball to rodeos, and often for nonsporting events as well. There are also specialized sports facilities such as racetracks of various types.

Some sporting facilities are owned by cities with major sports teams; others are privately owned. Even those owned or funded by municipalities are often run by a private management company, which handles the day-to-day management of the facility. Some private management companies are very large and manage facilities in different locales. Working for such a company can provide employees with a range of opportunities.

MANAGING THE FACILITY

The facility director is like the chief executive officer of the facility. He or she is responsible for the high-level direction of all activities that go into running the facility. The operations manager is at the center of the management of the facility, which includes overseeing the preparation of the facility for each event. The operations manager must also ensure that all equipment is maintained and repaired, and oversees the purchasing of supplies and equipment. The operations manager often supervises a large staff that includes both skilled and unskilled workers. The operations manager position requires technical knowledge of electrical and mechanical equipment as well as business and people skills. As in other sports areas, facilities often employ a public relations manager who is responsible for informing the public through the media of the sporting events being held at the facility. They also employ a box office manager, who supervises the sale of tickets, the accounting of the revenues generated, and special programs to promote ticket sales. Some facilities have a schedule of events for one team that plays there regularly. Others book different types of events. If this is the case, the facility will have a booking manager who arranges for events to be held at the facility. The booking manager spends most of his or her time talking to agents and promoters to arrange a successful roster of events for the facility.

Managing a large arena where college or professional sports are played is a high-pressure job that requires ensuring that events occur in smooth and safe fashion.

MANAGING EVENTS

The event director is responsible for overseeing the production of the actual events held at the facility. He or she supervises all the people required to put on the event, including ushers and technical personnel. He or she is the person who must resolve problems experienced by fans or participants in the sporting event. This position is important and exciting, but it is also very stressful. It is the event director who has to deal with unexpected problems and keep them from interfering with the event. One relatively

MANAGING CRISES IN SPORTS FACILITIES

Sports facilities managers have the opportunity to experience many exciting and exhilarating events. However, there are times when events take a negative turn and the responsibility for dealing with crises falls on the shoulders of the facility manager. Large numbers of people gather in sports facilities, along with high-profile athletes. For this reason, such facilities are at risk from criminals and some could be attractive targets for terrorists. In addition, natural disasters, such as hurricanes or tornadoes, could affect a facility.

Risk management is an area of facilities management that deals with reducing the chances of a crisis occurring during a sporting event. No matter how good security is at a sports facility, it is impossible to create an environment that is risk-free. Therefore, managers at sports facilities must be prepared to respond to, address, and direct recovery from crises with the least damage to fans, athletes, and the facility. The security manager is responsible for identifying potential threats and vulnerabilities in the facility. The security manager and the facility director must develop a plan to deal with emergencies, including who will respond; which emergency services and law enforcement agencies will be contacted, and by whom; and how spectators and participants will be evacuated from the facility, if necessary. If an emergency does occur, it is the job of the security team, under the direction of the security manager, to control the situation and ensure the safety of those present. Once the emergency is addressed, the public

(continued on next page)

(continued from previous page)

relations manager, in conjunction with the director of the facility, is responsible for informing the public of what has occurred, through the media. This is a critical function. How the occurrence is presented can have an effect on the reputation of the facility and the willingness of the public to use the facility in the future. The director's job does not end there, though. He or she must work with the facility's lawyers to deal with any legal issues that arise as a result of the event and must also consult with any inspectors or regulators who become involved in an investigation of the incident.

new administrative area that has arisen in recent years is game experience. The game experience coordinator is responsible for the digital devices that affect the viewers' experience during a sporting event. This person manages the images that are shown on video boards, music played during the event, and messaging that occurs during the game.

Facilities host large numbers of people and are therefore at risk of accidents—and, unfortunately, of deliberate crimes or acts of terrorism. The responsibility for keeping fans and participants safe falls to the security manager, who must evaluate each scheduled event to establish what risks might be associated with it and schedule appropriate personnel for crowd control. The security manager must be prepared to deal with any incidents that occur during

Mary Wittenberg, president and chief executive of the New York Road Runners (NYRR), oversees the New York City Marathon, among other races. As leader, she is responsible for an organization that also offers classes, maintains Web sites, publishes a magazine, and maintains a foundation that sponsors running programs for children.

sporting events. He or she must arrange for security cameras, adequate lighting, staffing of security stations that check fans' bags, and development of emergency response and evacuation plans. He or she also maintains relations with local law enforcement personnel who may be needed should an emergency arise.

Facility managers usually have a college degree in an area such as sports management or engineering. Many start out as entry-level administrative employees and work their way up to a higher level of responsibility. Those in security may have a degree or experience in law enforcement or risk management.

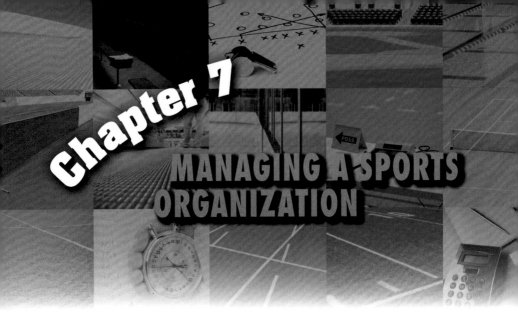

Sports at all levels are organized and regulated by industry organizations. There are major organizations that regulate semiprofessional, professional, and college sports, from the NCAA to the NBA. Other organizations provide services, training, and support to particular constituencies in sports. Coaches, sports tourism professionals, youth team directors and officials, and other groups have their own organizations as well. Within these organizations are specific areas devoted to the different types of activities and services the organization provides.

SPORTS ASSOCIATION MANAGEMENT AND ADMINISTRATION

A variety of management and administrative positions exist in associations at the state and national level that regulate youth, semipro, college, and professional sports activities. These organizations are usually composed of member teams or individuals. For example, the members of the NCAA are college teams, the members of the National Basketball Association are professional basketball teams, and so on.

These organizations perform various responsibilities for their members, which are carried out by different functional areas. Examples of such areas are:

- Fund-raising, which raises money for the organization's activities

- Training, which manages programs to train officials, coaches, or others

- Event production or scheduling of games, depending on the type of organization

- Communications, which is responsible for informing both members and the public of events and activities

- Membership, which is responsible for acquiring new members and dealing with issues that members have

- Compliance and enforcement, which is responsible for distributing information about regulations and ensuring that regulations are complied with

- Special projects, which is responsible for organizing events such as conferences that the organization produces

DEVELOPING A CAREER PLAN

To get where you want to go, you need a goal and a plan to achieve it. This is certainly true when it comes to your career. There are a variety of jobs in this field. How do you decide what type of career you want and what your ultimate goal is?

First, you need to make a list of your skills, interests, values, and personality traits. Next, you need to explore the different areas within sports management and administration and the different positions within those areas, matching the requirements of the job to your personal inventory. Then, you need to identify the educational institutions and internship or volunteer positions that will give you the training and experience you need to get a job in the area you want. Most sports management positions require an advanced degree. You must decide whether to go straight through school or work for such a degree part-time while working in the field at an entry-level job.

Once you have a job in the field, learn it thoroughly—and learn as much as you can about the next level. Take opportunities to acquire more responsibility. Keep honing your abilities both by continuing to learn in the field and by improving your general skills such as writing and dealing with conflict. Participate in industry organizations, which will help you make contacts that can keep you informed of opportunities and expose you to the different types of positions at the next level. Working for an industry organization also allows others to see you as a contributor to the industry. Once you understand where you could go from your present position, you can map out the next levels of jobs and prepare for them.

As with other sports management and administration jobs, managers and administrative staff in these areas generally require a college degree, and a graduate degree is desirable. The exact type of degree varies with the job, but examples include degrees in sports management, communications, finance, marketing, business, or public relations. Master's or Ph.D. degrees may be obtained in the same areas or business administration or law.

The director of rules and competition for the United States Golf Association supervises play at a golf championship. Ensuring that members comply with rules is essential for sports associations.

SPORTS COMMISSIONS

Sports commissions are a special type of sports organization, or league, charged with running the games for a particular sport or division of a sport. Major League Baseball (MLB) is an example of a commission. Commissions are headed by a commissioner, who is responsible for the control of the commission and for representing the commission to the public and press when necessary. Beneath the commissioner in the organization are a variety of

National Football League commissioner Roger Goodell appears onstage at the 2011 NFL Draft. Organizing the annual draft is one of the league's major responsibilities.

associate commissioners who are responsible for specific functional areas, such as specific sports at the college level or nonsports activities such as media relations, finance, legal affairs, operations, security, or special events. The responsibilities of managers and administrators in these positions are similar to those described earlier in this chapter. To succeed in most management and administrative positions in a commission requires knowledge of the league and the teams in it. It also requires a willingness to work long hours, which is often necessary during the playing season.

Chapter 8

NONSPORTS PROFESSIONALS IN SPORTS

This chapter covers the specialized areas that provide an opportunity for professionals to use their expertise in the world of sports. No industry can flourish without control of business aspects such as finance and law, and the area of sports is no exception. Because of the number and types of contracts involved in sports teams and events, these areas are of particular importance. For anyone who is planning to pursue a career as an accountant or lawyer and has an interest in sports, this can be an excellent way to combine those interests.

FINANCE

As should be apparent by now, ticket sales, media contracts, endorsements, and other aspects of sports generate millions of dollars. Therefore, financial management is a major issue for sports entities at all levels. Management and administrative positions in sports require a degree in finance or accounting. Some organizations may require that a candidate

Washington Nationals principal owner Mark Lerner (*left*) talks with Scott Boras, the agent who negotiated the contract for the team's number one draft pick in 2009. Boras has a law degree.

be an MBA in finance or accounting or a certified public accountant (CPA). The director of finance's or finance manager's job is to provide high-level oversight of the financial activities of the organization. He or she develops the budget for the organization, tracks revenues and expenses to ensure that the organization's finances remain in order, and invests the organization's funds. In addition, the finance manager carries out the financial planning of major expenditures such as building stadiums or purchasing capital equipment. The accounting manager is responsible for financial recordkeeping and for supervising accountants or accounting clerks who handle specific functions such as payroll and tracking receipts from tickets sales and expenditures.

LAW

The world of sports is full of legal issues and contracts. There are contracts with players, with sponsors, with vendors, with companies that want to make products with the name and logo of the sports team or event, and with the media who want to broadcast games or events. There are also a variety of legal issues that can arise as a result of putting on a sporting event. A sports organization may have to deal with legal claims relating to injuries, accidents, or property damage. All of these issues mean that a major sports organization must maintain either a legal staff or a relationship with a law firm that employs lawyers who specialize in sports. In addition to attorneys,

ETHICS IN SPORTS

Ethics is an important issue in sports. College and major league sports have been beset by numerous scandals, ranging from the treatment of women to the use of performance-enhancing drugs such as steroids. Sports managers are faced with numerous ethical issues they must be prepared to deal with. Among the issues that have arisen are:

- Gender and racial discrimination
- The use of Native American team nicknames and symbols
- Preferential treatment or awarding of unwarranted grades in academic subjects to star college athletes
- The appropriate age at which gymnasts should be allowed to compete because of the risk to their health
- The responsibility of teams to the communities in which they play
- The use of performance-enhancing drugs

Managers and administrators must be prepared to deal with pressure to make the team or players succeed at any cost. They must be ready to make and enforce policies that ensure ethical behavior. They must make others understand that violating ethical behavior can have serious consequences not just for the individuals involved but also for the team, and even the league, as a whole. The media are good at ferreting out unethical behavior. When news of a scandal is broken in the press, the

74

effects can be serious for the finances and the morale of the team. Allowing unethical behavior to occur has ruined many a career of managers as well as players. How does one ensure ethical behavior? See that others are treated the way you would like to be treated. Institute policies a reasonable person would consider acceptable. Do not allow violations of regulations or principles of the organization of which your team is a member. Allow only actions that you would feel comfortable having shown on TV or spread across the Internet. Above all, take swift action to address any violation of ethical principles on the part of staff or players.

sports organizations also employ legal assistants or paralegals who work with attorneys to prepare contracts and legal paperwork, and do legal research.

SPORTS AGENTS

Interesting opportunities exist in sports promotion management. Agents may work at sports management and marketing agencies or for individual sports. The agencies provide the opportunity to be involved in a variety of different events and work with a wide range of athletes and teams. Such careers offer a great deal of variety and are rarely boring. They can also be high-pressure careers because new events and projects are constantly coming up, and they have deadlines that must be met. Sports

Football star Chad Ochocinco meets with sports agent Drew Rosenhaus. Agents play a key role in managing sports stars' careers, negotiating their contracts with teams and sponsors.

management and marketing agencies provide representation, promotion, licensing, negotiating, marketing, or management services (or a combination of these) to athletes, teams, corporations, events, and even cities.

When representing an individual athlete client, representatives of the agency negotiate player contracts and product endorsement contracts, under which an athlete wears the logo of the product, and media contracts for commercials and TV or radio appearances. Agencies also promote and arrange product licensing for sports properties such as sports halls of fame or major sporting tours or events like college bowls. Similarly, they provide marketing and promotion services for major sporting events such as golf tournaments. Careers at such agencies include, among others, sponsorship sales agent, client representative, product placement agent, and market researcher. A sponsorship sales agent is responsible for obtaining financial backing from corporations for sporting events. Client representatives negotiate contracts and solicit promotional opportunities and endorsements for clients. Product placement is a service that works with motion picture producers to get sports entities such as NASCAR featured in movies, which is a means of advertising the product. Market researchers conduct surveys through the mail, online, or via focus groups to obtain feedback that will help make sporting events successful. These positions generally require a degree in sports management, business, or communications.

Chapter 9

MANAGING SPORTS TOURISM AND FITNESS

Sports tourism activities range from managing activities on cruise ships to organizing sports-related adventure trips for tourists and amateur athletes. Sports tourists includes visitors who travel to participate in a sport such as skiing or golf as well as visitors who travel to view sports.

SPORTS TOURISM

Some tourists seek sport as part of a vacation that includes other activities. For example, they may travel to a resort or on cruise ship, where they ski or play tennis as well as engage in other non-sports-related activities such as sightseeing. Other tourists travel explicitly for the purpose of participating in a golf tournament, for example, or a biking or hiking trip. The interest in sports-focused vacations has led some locales to sponsor sports package vacations—for instance, the Yellowstone National Park's Yellowstone on Skis vacation and Key Largo, Florida's, Water Sports vacation package.

At sea, a cruise ship's sports director (*left*) is with a guest at the outdoor recreation area, a suspended ropes course of rope bridges and swinging steps and beams. Today's tourists often seek exciting and challenging sporting activities while on vacation.

Sports management positions in sports tourism include tournament planner and cruise line sports director. Tournament planners are responsible for making all the arrangements for a tournament. They must supervise the individuals responsible for various aspects of the tournament, often over several days. Tournament planners generally require at least a bachelor's degree in sports management, recreation, leisure, tourism, or a related area.

Cruise line sports and fitness directors are responsible for planning and managing sports and fitness activities on board a cruise ship. They design the sports and fitness program, supervise the fitness staff, and plan special on-board sports events such as water polo tournaments. A bachelor's degree in recreation or sports management is usually required.

FITNESS

Fitness directors at resorts perform similar functions, planning fitness activities and supervising the fitness staff and pros who provide instruction to guests. Like the head of any other department at a resort, they must control the budget and track expenses for their department. If the resort charges for sports lessons, they must oversee the promotion of the sports activities at the resort and track revenues. They must also make sure that all the sports equipment and facilities are adequately maintained.

An assistant golf professional (*left*) at a Florida resort gives putting lessons to a golfer. Many resorts employ golf professionals to offer lessons at the golf driving range or putting greens. Resort management includes supervision of sports activities and revenues.

While not part of the tourist industry per se, sports clubs are a related industry. There are many different types of fitness and sports clubs, ranging from general gyms to golf clubs to tennis clubs, as well as public facilities. The growth in the number of chains in the fitness industry, such as LA Fitness, Gold's Gym, and Curves, among others, has created a number of corporate positions not

DEALING WITH PEOPLE FROM OTHER CULTURES

Tourists and travelers come from all over the world, and adventure travel can lead a tour group from the United States and Canada to a foreign destination. For this reason, those engaged in sports tourism must be prepared to deal in an effective way with people from other cultures. It is important to be aware of how people from other cultures are responding to your speech and behavior. What is considered amusing by Americans may be offensive to people from other cultures. Treat people as individuals, and avoid stereotyping them. Ask people how they would like to be addressed. Avoid touching people from other cultures, especially women. Be aware that gestures have different meanings in different cultures. Often, showing knowledge of their language or culture will make people feel more at ease. However, be careful not to sound patronizing. Treat everyone with respect.

managing an individual club but overseeing the management of a group of clubs or franchises, at the corporate or district level.

ADVENTURE MANAGEMENT

Adventure travel is a special subset of sports tourism. Adventure travel includes trips taken in order to experience athletic activities in the natural environment, combining elements of sports and adventure. Examples include white water rafting or mountaineering trips. Firms that offer adventure travel experiences require adventure travel leaders

White-water rafting is an example of adventure travel. Leading such trips requires the ability to manage participants with different levels of skills and to deal with unexpected problems.

and coordinators. Those in these positions must be trained and experienced in both the sport of choice and tourism skills. They plan trips, including both the sports activities and the arrangements necessary for the overall trip, such as accommodations and equipment. This can be a great career for someone who is adventurous and likes working out of doors. It is important to remember, however, that the job requires the coordinator to spend a great deal of time on careful planning to ensure both the satisfaction and the safety of the participants. It also requires the ability to handle a variety of problems ranging from lost room reservations to physical injury. This position generally requires at least a bachelor's degree in sports management, recreation, or tourism. It also requires excellent physical fitness and experience and/or certification in the types of activities in which the participants will be engaging.

Chapter 10

MANAGING SPORTING SPECIAL EVENTS

Sporting special events include major marathons, extreme sports events, and national and international competitions. The most renowned special sporting event is, of course, the Olympics. Sports management positions exist in agencies involved in producing sporting events and in organizations assembled to produce a particular one-time event. Sporting special events can be local, national, or international. They can range from a city marathon to a statewide tennis competition to a national skateboarding championship to a World Cup ski race. Depending on the scope of the event, an individual may be hired to coordinate and manage the planning and production of the event, or an agency may be hired to handle these functions. Individuals can find management and administrative positions at sporting event agencies, events that have permanent staff, or charities that maintain an event staff because they regularly produce events to raise money.

Long before the runners hit the road, special events planners make major preparations to ensure that a marathon can be held successfully. Planning includes having police, paramedics, water supplies, and portable toilets at the ready.

SPORTS AGENCIES

Many sports agencies handle only particular aspects of a sporting event. In this case, a director or producer will be hired to manage the overall production of the event. This person oversees the planning of the event and choosing the agencies that are responsible for various aspects of the production. He or she may also hire individuals who are in charge of particular tasks at the event, such as security or ushering.

PARTICIPATING IN INTERNATIONAL EVENTS

The sports industry, like most other industries today, has become global. Major events take place in venues around the world that involve personnel from various countries. Also, major events produced in North America may involve athletes and officials from around the world. In particular, major sports agencies with recognized expertise may be called on to participate in producing events in other countries. Working in international sports—either at an organization such as the Fédération Internationale de Football Association (International Soccer Association) or at a company that is involved in producing international sporting events—requires knowledge of international business. This means familiarizing yourself with the regulations, services, personnel practices, and financial processes of the locale in which you will be working.

In addition to the usual sports management skills required, speaking the language of the area in which you will be working is extremely important. Therefore, if you are interested in an international career in sports, it is a good idea to learn one or more languages other than your native one. Even better is first-hand experience of other cultures. If you are seriously interested in pursuing a career in international sports, you should consider a semester abroad as an exchange student or a summer internship in another country. When you work abroad, even on a temporary project, putting on a sporting event, you must adapt to the culture, business methods, and laws of the locale in which you work. So it is crucial to familiarize yourself with these.

Although some agencies handle the complete production of special sports events, most specialize in a particular aspect, such as marketing, event development, event management, soliciting sponsors, or television production. Full-service agencies are most commonly used for major sporting events such as national golf tournaments or auto races sponsored by a major corporation. Full-service agencies handle all aspects of the event from planning through broadcasting. They also often have divisions that handle promotion and licensing for sports franchises and individual athletes.

Security guards screen fans before Super Bowl XLIV between the Indianapolis Colts and New Orleans Saints in 2010. Security is a major concern at high-profile special events.

Positions at such agencies frequently pay well and provide the opportunity to participate in the production of high-profile events and work with well-known athletes. They are often high-pressure jobs that require long hours leading up to and during the event with tight deadlines and the ability to handle many issues at once.

Specialized agencies either provide a particular service or work with particular types of clients. For example, an agency may specialize in arranging corporate sponsorships for sporting events, which can be very satisfying work because it helps make an event possible. Or a specialized agency may provide broadcast services for sporting events.

Major annual events and tours maintain their own staff and often engage in activities such as licensing, sponsorship solicitation, and fund-raising year-round. However, because the event itself is seasonal, only a small staff may be maintained full-time, with the staff being supplemented by additional personnel and agencies hired while the event is actively being produced. Some charities produce events such as races around the country on a regular basis as part of their fund-raising efforts. In this case, they may maintain a permanent staff to handle the financial management, planning, and execution of events, supplemented by local personnel hired at the time of the event.

SPORTING EVENT MANAGEMENT AND ADMINISTRATION

Planning and running a major sporting event is a huge responsibility, but even small events require a great deal of planning. Permits must be obtained, venues rented or arranged, viewing areas or stands arranged for, and security, food vendors, and cleanup crews hired. Appropriate arrangements must be made for participants, and publicity on the event must be generated. If it is a major event, broadcast and press arrangements must also be made and media coordination has to be performed. In addition, local law enforcement and medical services must be coordinated so they are available in case of need. All sporting events require a significant management and administrative staff in finance, security, tournament operations, registration, volunteer management, and marketing and publicity. The head of the event is called the producer or executive director. He or she is responsible for the overall management of the event. Below this person are other management personnel, who are responsible for particular areas.

FINANCE AND OPERATIONS

To make money through a special event, the first step is to make a budget. Expenses and income must be tracked against the budget to ensure that the event remains on a firm footing. This is the responsibility of the finance manager and the accounting staff.

Whereas the finance manager keeps the event running behind the scenes, the operations director or manager is responsible for the activities necessary to stage the event. This person and his or her administrative staff must make sure the physical facilities and equipment are in the proper condition for the event, oversee the schedule of activities, arrange signage, hire food and beverage staff or vendors, and arrange and oversee merchandise sales. They must arrange housing and transportation for athletes and transportation

The tournament director for the PGA Tour surveys activities at a major competition. To ensure that a tournament is successful, the director must guarantee that everything goes according to plan.

such as shuttle buses to nearby hotels for fans. They arrange facilities for broadcast media and the press, plan and arrange communications for staff, work with security on crowd control and security issues, and coordinate with the communications staff on publicity and public relations. The operations director prepares a detailed "script" that covers what's supposed to happen throughout the entire event and then uses this as a roadmap to make sure that equipment and personnel are where they are needed at the appropriate time. The operations staff members are assigned to individual activities to make sure everything is set up and to deal with any issues that arise. After the event is over, operations is responsible for seeing to the teardown and storage of equipment and signs, cleanup of the venue, and follow-up with vendors and other entities involved in the event.

Operations is the broadest area, and those who do this job must be prepared to work long hours on tight deadlines and deal with a wide range of vendors, staff, outside agencies, athletes, and personnel from facilities around the venue, such as hotels. It can be very satisfying, however, because when the event occurs, those who work in this area know they are personally responsible for making the event a success. Under operations are a number of different areas with particular responsibilities. Some of these positions are similar to those in other areas of sports. Some, however, are unique to special events.

Special sporting events bring individual partici- pants together to compete. Hence, a system of register- ing participants is necessary. The registration manager and staff are the first point of contact for athletes partic- ipating in the event. Many events incorporate advanced registration for participants, which may be done in a va- riety of ways. One of the most common today is to allow people to register over the Internet. Major events such as the World Cup and the Olympics, however, may require greater personal contact with participant organizations prior to arrival. It is the job of the registration man- ager to develop a system for registering participants. If the system incorporates Internet access, he or she may work with the information systems manager and staff to make sure an online system is created that captures the necessary information. The registration manager must develop a plan that determines the information and fees that must be gathered from participants and the con- firmations that must be provided after registration, as well as any post-registration information such as in- formation on transportation, housing, and schedules. If the event includes minors, it may also be necessary to arrange for parental consent forms. The registration manager must also supervise on-site registration staff during the event and field any problems such as lost reg- istration information.

Volunteer management is an important aspect of most special sports events, especially those occurring at the local and state level. Even major events such as the Olympics rely on volunteers to supplement their staff. A major source of volunteers is students who wish to gain experience in sports administration. The volunteer manager has a demanding but rewarding job. He or she is dealing with a large number of people who are largely inexperienced in the tasks they are performing. The volunteer manager works with the other operational managers to establish where and how many volunteers are needed. He or she then must recruit volunteers, using a variety of means of getting the word out. This can include contacting high schools or colleges; posting notices in print media or on appropriate Web sites, including the event's own site; and using social media such as Twitter or Facebook. The volunteer manager must see that the volunteers are trained both in their specific jobs and in how to handle problems that might arise. Finally, the volunteer manager must schedule and supervise the volunteers.

The success of any sporting event depends on getting people to attend it, and this is the job of marketing. Event marketing managers and staff are responsible for advertising, public relations, broadcasting, licensing and selling of branded merchandise, corporate sponsorship, and fundraising. In a large event, there may be a different manager and staff in each of these areas.

Security and maintaining order at international sporting events can sometimes be challenging. Passion can run high among fans at special events, and security must be ready to deal with violence or even a riot.

RISK MANAGEMENT AND SECURITY

There are two aspects to protecting the event, its sponsors, and its participants—risk management and security. The risk manager is responsible for ensuring that the chance of dangerous incidents and accidents occurring is minimized and for ensuring that adequate preventative measures and insurance are in place so that the event and its sponsors are protected against lawsuits. The responsibilities of the risk manager and his or her staff are to evaluate the venue and activities to establish where risks may lie, and then to put precautionary measures in place to minimize the chance that a problem will occur. The areas covered can include everything from preparing legal waivers for volunteers and participants to ensuring that lighting is adequate in areas that participants and fans have to cross.

A related area is the physical protection of the participants, staff, volunteers, and fans. This is the venue of the security manager. Security can range from hiring off-duty policemen at a local event to employing a full-service security firm at a major national tournament. The job of the security staff includes making sure that fans do not bring dangerous items into the venue; that areas where fans or participants are located are adequately patrolled, so that they are protected from criminals and, in the case of high-profile events, terrorists; and working with local law enforcement to ensure that an appropriate response is quickly available if there is a problem. The security manager is also responsible for drawing up an emergency response plan in case a problem does occur during the event. For those interested in a career in security, sports can provide an interesting and exciting area in which to employ one's skills.

QUALIFICATIONS FOR EVENT MANAGEMENT AND ADMINISTRATION

Managerial and often administrative positions in event production require a degree in sports management, event management, marketing, or finance, depending on the area one is interested in working in. Some positions such as security may require specialized training or experience in security or law enforcement. Courses in tourism and hospitality or recreational management may also be useful, especially for operational management and administrative positions. These types of courses provide information on managing events in general that is applicable to sporting events. An internship or experience as a volunteer at sporting events is an excellent way to gain experience that can help one gain an entry-level position in this field. Because special events are, by definition, one-time occurrences, there is no chance for potential employers to observe how you perform and then decide whether you're right for a position, as there is in a regular job. Being able to show that you have already performed the activities required is, therefore, very important in obtaining a position in event management and administration.

COLLEGE AND UNIVERSITY PROGRAMS IN SPORTS MANAGEMENT AND ADMINISTRATION

The following is a list of a number of colleges and universities that offered programs in sports management and administration at the time of writing:

Alderson-Broaddus College, Philippi, WV: bachelor's degree in recreational sports management

American InterContinental University, Hoffman Estates, IL: master's degree in business administration–sports management

American Military University, Charles Town, WV: master's degree in sports management

Aquinas College, Grand Rapids, MI: bachelor's and master's degrees in Business administration–sports Management

Arcadia University, Glenside, PA: bachelor's degree in sports management

Arkansas State University, Jonesboro, AR: bachelor's degree in sports management

Augustana College, Sioux Falls, SD: bachelor's degree in sports management

Baldwin Wallace College, Berea, OH: bachelor's degree in sports management

Ball State University, Muncie, IN: bachelor's degree in sports administration

Barry University, Miami Shores, FL: bachelor's degree in sports management

Baylor University, Waco, TX: master's degree in sports management

Becker College, Worcester, MA: bachelor's degree in business administration–sports management

Bellevue University, Bellevue, NE: bachelor's degree in sports management

Bethany University, Scotts Valley, CA: bachelor's degree in sports management

Bowie State University, Bowie, MD: bachelor's degree in sports management

Bowling Green State University, Bowling Green, OH: bachelor's and master's degrees in sports management, recreation and tourism, leisure, and event planning

Brock University, St. Catharines, ON, Canada: bachelor's, master's, and Ph.D. degrees in sports management

Brooklyn College, Brooklyn, NY: master's degree in physical education–sports management

California State University, Long Beach, CA: master's degree in sports management

Canisius College, Buffalo, NY: master's degree in sports administration

Canton State University of New York, Canton, NY: bachelor's degree in sports management

Cardinal Stritch University, Milwaukee, WI: master's degree in sports management

Carroll College, Helena, MT: bachelor's degree in health and physical education–sports management

Catholic University, Washington, DC: bachelor's degree in business and economics–sports management

Chadron State College, Chadron, NE: master's degree in organizational management–sports management

The Citadel, Charleston, SC: master's degree in business administration–sports management

Colorado Mesa University, Grand Junction, CO: bachelor's degree in sports management, master's degree in sports management

Columbia College, Columbia, MO: bachelor's degree in sports management

Columbia Southern University, Orange Beach, AL: bachelor's degree in business administration–sports management

Columbia University, New York, NY: master's degree in sports management

Concord College, Athens, WV: bachelor's degree in sports management

Concordia University, Chicago, IL: bachelor's degree in sports management

Concordia University, Irvine, CA: bachelor's degree in sports management, master's degree in coaching and athletic administration

Concordia University, St. Paul, MN: master's degree in sports management

Coppin State University, Baltimore, MD: bachelor's degree in sports management

Cornerstone University, Grand Rapids, MI: bachelor's

degree in business–sports management

Cowley College, Arkansas City, KS: associate's degree in sports management–sports administration

Culver-Stockton College, Canton, MO: bachelor's degree in sports management

Dakota Wesleyan University, Mitchell, SD: bachelor's degree in sports management

Daniel Webster College, Nashua, NH: bachelor's degree in sports management

DePaul University, Chicago, IL: master's degree in sports management

Dowling College, Oakdale, NY: bachelor's degree in sports management

Drexel University, Philadelphia, PA: master's degree in sports management

Eastern Michigan University, Ypsilanti, MI: master's degree in sports management

Eastern New Mexico University, Portales, NM: master's degree in sports administration and sport science

East Stroudsburg University, East Stroudsburg, PA: master's degree in management and leadership in sports management

Emmanuel College, Franklin Springs, GA: bachelor's degree in sports management

Endicott College, Beverly, MA: bachelor's degree in sport management

Faulkner University, Montgomery, AL: bachelor's degree in physical education and sports management

Ferris State University, Big Rapids, MI: bachelor's degree in recreation leadership and management

Finger Lakes Community College, Canandaigua, NY: associate's degree in sports and tourism studies

Finlandia University, Hancock, MI: bachelor's degree in sports management

Flagler College, St. Augustine, FL: bachelor's degree in sports management

Florida Atlantic University, Boca Raton, FL: master's degree in sports management

Florida College, Temple Terrace, FL: bachelor's degree in business administration–sports management

Florida Institute of Technology, Melbourne, FL: bachelor's degree in sports management

Florida State University, Tallahassee, FL: bachelor's, master's, and Ph.D. degrees in sports management

Fontbonne University, St. Louis, MO: bachelor's degree in sports management

Fort Hays State University, Hays, KS: bachelor's degree in physical education–recreation and sports management

Franklin Pierce University, Rindge, NH: master's degree in sports management

Gannon University, Erie, PA: bachelor's degree in sports management and marketing

Georgetown University, Washington, DC: master's degree in sports industry management

George Washington University, Washington, DC: master's degree in sports management

Goldey-Beacom College, Wilmington, DE: bachelor's degree in business administration–sports management

Greenville College, Greenville, IL: bachelor's degree in recreation–sports management

Hampden-Sydney College, Hampden-Sydney, VA: bachelor's and master's degrees in sports management

Harcum College, Bryn Mawr, PA: bachelor's degree in sports management

Howard University, Washington, DC: bachelor's degree in sport management

Husson University, Bangor, ME: bachelor's degree in business–sports management

Indiana State University, Terre Haute, IN: bachelor's and master's degrees in sports management, and recreation and youth leadership

Indiana Tech, Fort Wayne, IN: bachelor's degree in business administration–sports management

Indiana University, Bloomington, IN: bachelor's, master's, and Ph.D. degrees in athletic administration and sports management

Indiana University of Pennsylvania, Indiana, PA: bachelor's degree in sports administration

Indiana Wesleyan University, Marion, IN: bachelor's degree in sports management

Jacksonville University, Jacksonville, FL: bachelor's and master's degrees in sports management

Johnson & Wales University, Providence, RI: bachelor's degree in sports management

Judson University, Elgin, IL: bachelor's degree in

exercise and sport science–sports administration

Kansas Wesleyan University, Salina, KS: master's degree in sports management

Kent State University, Kent, OH: bachelor's and master's degrees in sports administration, and sports and recreation management

Kentucky Wesleyan College, Owensboro, KY: bachelor's and master's degrees in fitness and sports management

Lasell College, Newton, MA: bachelor's and master's degrees in sports management

Lenoir-Rhyne University, Hickory, NC: bachelor's degree in sports management

LeTourneau University, Longview, TX: bachelor's degree in kinesiology–sports management

Liberty University, Lynchburg, VA: bachelor's and master's degrees in sports management

Limestone College, Gaffney, SC: bachelor's degree in sports management

Lindenwood University, St. Charles, MO: bachelor's degree in sports management

Lone Star College, The Woodlands, TX: master's degree in sports management

Loras College, Dubuque, IA: bachelor's degree in sports management

Louisiana State University, Baton Rouge, LA: bachelor's and master's degrees in sports management

Loyola University, Chicago, IL: master's degree in sports management

Lynn University, Boca Raton, FL: bachelor's degree in sports management and master's degree in sports and athletics administration

Madonna University, Livonia, MI: bachelor's degree in sports management

Marietta College, Marietta, OH: bachelor's degree in sports management

Maryville University, St. Louis, MO: bachelor's degree in sports business management

Mayville State University, Mayville, ND: bachelor's degree in sports management

Merrimac College, North Andover, MA: bachelor's degree in sports management

Messiah College, Grantham, PA: bachelor's degree in sports management

Methodist University, Fayetteville, NC: bachelor's degree in business–sports management

Michigan State University, East Lansing, MI: master's degree in sports administration

MidAmerica Nazarene College, Olathe, KS: bachelor's degree in sports management

Midway College, Midway, KY: bachelor's degree in sports management

Minnesota State University, Mankato, MN: master's degree in sports management

Misericordia University, Dallas, PA: bachelor's degree in sports management

Mississippi State University, Mississippi State, MS: master's degree in sports management

Missouri State University, Springfield, MO: master's degree in sports management

Mitchell College, London, CT: bachelor's degree in sports and fitness management

Mount Ida College, Newton, MA: bachelor's degree in sports management

New York University, New York, NY: bachelor's degree in sports management

North Carolina State University, Raleigh, NC: bachelor's degree in sports management

North Central University, Minneapolis, MN: bachelor's degree in sports management

Northcentral University, Prescott Valley, AZ: master's degree in athletic

administration and a
Ph.D. in athletic administration

Northwestern University,
Chicago, IL: master's degree
in sports administration

Ohio State University,
Columbus, OH: master's
and Ph.D. degrees in
sports management

Ohio University, Athens, OH:
master's degree in athletic
administration and master's
degree in coaching
education

Ohio Valley University,
Vienna, WV: bachelor's
degree in sports management

Oklahoma State University,
Stillwater, OK: bachelor's
degree in management–
sports management

Old Dominion University,
Norfolk, VA: bachelor's and
master's degrees in sports
management

Point Park University, Pitts-
burgh, PA: bachelor's and
master's degrees in sports,
arts and entertainment
management

Purdue University, West
Lafayette, IN: master's
degree in recreation
and sports management

Regis College, Weston, MA:
bachelor's degree in sports
management

Rice University, Houston, TX:
bachelor's degree in sports
management

Rutgers University, New
Brunswick, NJ:
bachelor's degree in
sports management

St. Bonaventure University,
St. Bonaventure, NY:
bachelor's degree in
sports studies–sports
management

St. Cloud State University,
St. Cloud, MN: bachelor's
degree in recreation–sports
managemen

St. John Fisher College, Roch-
ester, NY: bachelor's degree
in sports management

St. John's University, Queens,
NY: bachelor's degree in
sport management and
master's degree in sports
management

St. Thomas Aquinas College, Sparkill, NY: bachelor's degree in sports management

St. Thomas University, Miami Gardens, FL: master's degree in sports administration

Sam Houston State University, Huntsville, TX: master's degree in kinesiology–sports management

San Diego State University, San Diego, CA: master's degree in sports business management

Seton Hall University, South Orange, NJ: bachelor's and master's degrees in sports management

Seton Hill University, Greensburg, PA: bachelor's degree in sports management

Shawnee State University, Portsmouth, OH: bachelor's degree in sports studies–sports management

Shorter University, Rome, GA: bachelor's degree in sports management

Southeast Missouri State University, Cape Girardeau, MO: bachelor's degree in sports management

Southern Methodist University, Dallas, TX: bachelor's and master's degrees in sports management

Southern Vermont College, Bennington, VT: bachelor's degree in business administration–sports management

Southwest Baptist University, Bolivar, MO: bachelor's degree in sports management

Southwest Minnesota State University, Marshall, MN: bachelor's degree in sports management

State University of New York, Cortland, NY: bachelor's degree in sports management

Stetson University, DeLand, FL: bachelor's degree in sports management and master's degree in sports management

Temple University, Philadelphia, PA: master's degree in sports and recreation management

Texas A&M University, College Station, TX: bachelor's, master's, and Ph.D. degrees in sports management

Texas Woman's University, Denton, TX: master's degree in sports management

Tiffin University, Tiffin, OH: master's degree in sports management

University of Arkansas, Fayetteville, AR: bachelor's degree in recreation and sport management, master's degree in recreation and sports management

University of Connecticut, Storrs, CT: bachelor's, master's, and Ph.D. degrees in sports management

University of Florida, Gainesville, FL: bachelor's, master's, and Ph.D. degrees in sports management

University of Indianapolis, Indianapolis, IN: bachelor's degree in sports management

University of Massachusetts, Amherst, MA: bachelor's, master's, and Ph.D. degrees in sports management

University of Michigan, Ann Arbor, MI: bachelor's degree in sports management

University of New England, Biddeford and Portland, ME: bachelor's degree in sports management

University of New Haven, West Haven, CT: bachelor's degree in management of sports industries

The University of North Carolina, Chapel Hill, NC: bachelor's degree in exercise and sports science–sports administration

University of North Florida, Jacksonville, FL: bachelor's degree in sports management

University of Ottawa, Ottawa ON, Canada: bachelor's, master's, and Ph.D. degrees in sports management

University of Saint Mary, Leavenworth, KS: bachelor's degree in sports management

University of San Francisco, San Francisco, CA: master's degree in sports management

The University of Tampa, Tampa, FL: bachelor's degree in sports management

The University of Texas, Austin, TX: bachelor's, master's, and Ph.D. degrees in sports management

University of Utah, Lake City, UT: bachelor's degree in community recreation and sports management

Urbana University, Urbana, OH: bachelor's degree in sports management

Waldorff College, Forest City, IA: bachelor's degree in sports management

Wartburg College, Waverly, IA: bachelor's degree in business administration–sports management

Washington State University, Pullman, WA: master's degree in sports management

Willmington College, Willmington, OH: bachelor's degree in sports management

Wilmington College, New Castle, DE: bachelor's degree in sports management

Winona State University, Winona, MN: master's degree in sports management

Winthrop University, Rock Hill, SC: bachelor's degree in sports management

York College, York, NE: bachelor's degree in sports management

The following colleges offer online programs:

American Military University, Charles Town, WV: master's degree in sports management

American Public University, Charles Town, WV: master's degree in sports

management, graduate certificate in sports management, graduate certificate in athletic administration

Ashford University, Clinton, IA: bachelor's degree in

sports and recreation management

California University at Pennsylvania Online, California, PA: bachelor's degree in sports management, master's degree in sports management studies

Drexel University, Philadelphia, PA: master's degree in sports management

Full Sail University, Winter Park, FL: master's degree in sports management

Grand Canyon University, Phoenix, AZ: bachelor's degree in business administration–sports management

Lasell College, Newtonville, MA: master's degree in sports management (concentrations in sports leadership, sports hospitality, or sports non-profit)

Liberty University, Lynchburg, VA: master's degree in sports management

Northeastern University, Boston, MA: master's degree in sports leadership

Post University, Waterbury, CT: bachelor's degree in sports management

St. Leo University, Saint Leo, FL: master's degree in sports business

Southern New Hampshire University, Manchester, NH: bachelor's degree in sports management

Southern New Hampshire University Online, Manchester, NH: master's degree in sports management

Tiffin University, Tiffin, OH: bachelor's degree in business administration in sports and recreation management

Some possible career paths and their descriptions include the following:

- Sports management and administration is the planning and execution of all the functions necessary to run a sports team, facility, organization, or event.

- Sports management and administration jobs exist at the high school, college, semiprofessional, and professional level.

- Most sports management and administration positions require a college degree, either in sports management or administration, or in business, communications, information technology, finance, or law.

- For managerial positions, it is beneficial to have a master's degree, either in sports management or in business administration.

- Practical experience is of great help when looking for a job in sports management and administration.

- Experience can be gained by volunteer work with youth or semipro teams or sporting events.

- Internships during college can provide one with valuable experience and contacts.

- At the top of the college sports hierarchy is the athletics director, who may have a number of assistant directors, each of whom is responsible for a specific area, such as media relations, compliance, ticket sales, marketing, facilities, events, fund-raising or development, accounting, and finance.

- Many universities now have a dedicated women's athletic administrator or director, who is in charge of the women's sports program.

- Managerial and administrative areas in college athletics include athletic development, facilities, ticket sales, finance, compliance, student athlete services, community relations, public relations, media relations, and championships and special events.

- Managerial and administrative positions in college conference organizations include enforcement and compliance, marketing, championship administration, public relations, officiating, and broadcasting.

- In professional sports, managerial and administrative positions exist in general management, scouting, human resources, and player education.

- The stadium manager and staff are responsible for the upkeep of the physical building and playing area where the sport takes place.

- Communication positions in professional sports include video coordinator, public relations manager, and community relations manager and their staffs.

- Managerial and administrative positions in professional sports also exist in ticket sales, corporate sales, finance, and information technology.

- The facility manager is the chief executive of a sports facility.

- The operations manager is in charge of all the activities required to put on an event at the facility. He or she has staff that handles a variety of specific areas.

- Facilities employ box office, booking, public relations, and security management and administrative personnel.

- The event manager handles the actual production of events, including supervising personnel such as ushers and technical staff.

- The game experience manager uses audio and video technologies to enhance viewers' experience of a sporting event.

- Organizations that organize and regulate sport at all levels require managerial and administrative personnel in areas such as fund-raising, training, event production and game scheduling, membership, compliance, and special projects.

- Professionals with degrees in areas such as finance and law are required by sports organizations and teams.

- Sports agents represent athletes and negotiate with teams and sponsors on their behalf.

- Sports tourism and adventure travel provide managerial and administrative positions on cruise ships, in resorts, and leading groups of tourists on sporting activities.

- Sporting events at the local, national, and international level require a significant management and administrative staff in finance, security, tournament operations, registration, volunteer management, risk management and security, and marketing and publicity.

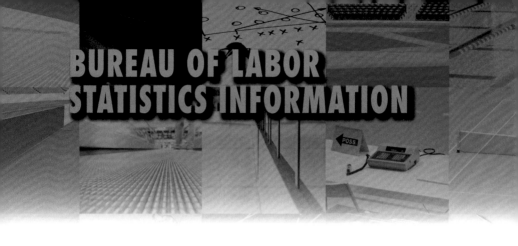

According to the U.S. Bureau of Labor Statistics (BLS), annual job growth in managerial positions of the type that occur in sports is expected to average 3 to 4 percent. However, the bureau does not break out sports management and administration separately from general managerial and administrative jobs. Nevertheless, the bureau predicts that in general jobs for athletes, coaches, officials, and those in related positions should increase faster than the average job market through 2018. This should mean that there would continue to be a steady demand for those who manage and administer sports. The bureau points out, however, that competition for athletic jobs will be keen.

The bureau foresees an increase in the number of people participating in organized sports, and as the number of retirees grows, a rise in the number of people who participate in recreational sports activity. The bureau anticipates these factors to increase the demand for personnel involved in sports activities. The bureau envisions an expansion in college sports, especially in the area of women's sports. Future expansion of sports teams is also expected to create additional jobs.

SPORTS MANAGEMENT

According to the BLS information on sport coaches, officials, and related jobs, 52 percent of those in wage and salaried jobs in sports are employed in educational venues, and approximately 13 percent work in the amusement and recreation industries, including health clubs, martial arts studios, gyms, riding stables, and golf, swim, and tennis clubs. About 6 percent work in spectator sports. Roughly 16 percent are self-employed. They work as scouts, officials, and instructors for various sports. The BLS sees faster growth in the sports industry than the average for all occupations. However, competition for jobs at the highest levels of sports is expected to be intense. Those seeking positions with women's sports teams will face less competition. As mentioned previously, the increase in the number of retirees who want to participate in leisure sports is expected to lead to more job opportunities in this field. In addition, the demand of parents who want athletic training for their children and the formation of new sports teams and leagues in the future are expected to contribute to job growth. Cities with many colleges and professional sports teams provide the greatest opportunity for finding a job in this field. Population growth is expected to be the greatest in the West and South, so those areas may see an expansion in job opportunities.

ACADEMIC SPORTS ADMINISTRATION

The BLS expects population growth to lead to an increase in the number of schools. The poor economic conditions may restrict money for schools, but the popularity of sports is expected to still lead to an increase in the number of school-based positions in sports. According to the BLS, 35 percent of academic administrators worked more than forty hours per week, including supervising activities on evenings and weekends. This is likely to be the case with college athletics directors. Most academic administrators have a master's or Ph.D. degree. Advancement for academic administrators, including those in sports, usually takes the form of moving to a larger or more prestigious institution. As with other high-level college and university positions, athletics directors may have to apply to a variety of colleges and accept a position wherever there is a job opening. Thus, like professional athletics, the availability of a position will dictate the location in which they work. In general, the growth rate for academic administrators is expected to mirror the average for all professions.

FITNESS AND HEALTH

Fitness workers, including fitness directors and supervisors, work at health clubs, gyms, and recreational facilities. The growing concern with obesity, especially among young people, is expected to increase demand for services in the fitness area. Many employers spend money on fitness in offering their employees programs to help them stay healthy and in good shape. The BLS anticipates faster than average job growth in the fitness industry, with growth of 29 percent from 2008 to 2018.

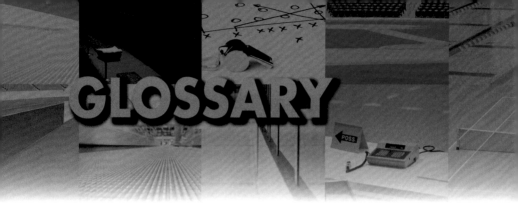

accessibility Ability to be easily approached or entered.

aerial Taking place in the air; in sports, involving tricks in the air.

agent A representative of a player who performs activities such as soliciting endorsements and negotiating contracts.

attire Clothing.

avid Enthusiastic; keenly interested.

beneficial Helpful.

blog A journal maintained on the Internet and available to the public.

community relations A business area that deals with maintaining a positive relationship with the people who live in the area where a team plays.

compliance Following of the rules.

demeanor Appearance.

draft A procedure whereby new or existing sports players are made available for selection or reselection by the teams in a league.

eligibility Being qualified or entitled to be chosen for something.

endorsement In sports, money paid to an athlete by a company to promote the company's product.

entail Involve.

entree The act of entering.

equal opportunity The policy of treating employees and others without discrimination, especially on the basis of their sex, race, or age.

expenditures Money paid out for expenses.

explicit Fully and clearly expressed.

hierarchy An organization with the individual positions ranked from highest to lowest.

hone Sharpen.

incentive A special promotion or discount designed to stimulate an increase in sales.

inhospitable Providing a harsh and difficult environment; not friendly.

legal Relating to the law.

mandate An official order to do something; the authority to carry out a policy or course of action.

negotiate Bargain with another person or persons to arrive at an agreement.

project management The process of overseeing all the elements of a project to ensure that it meets its goals.

prowess Skill.

public relations A business area that deals with getting information on a team or event to the public, usually through print or broadcast media.

revenue Money earned.

segment A portion of an industry engaged in a particular type or level of activity.

sexual harassment Harassment, usually of a woman, in a workplace or other professional or social situation, involving the making of unwanted sexual advances or obscene remarks.

social media An electronic application or Web site that allows members to exchange information about themselves with others.

software Computer programs, such as those that track the phases of a project and the resources used.

solicit Ask someone for something.

syntax The rules that govern how sentences are constructed in a language.

vendor A person or company that supplies goods or services.

venue A location or area.

Amateur Athletic Union
1910 Hotel Plaza Boulevard
Lake Buena Vista, FL 32830
(407) 934-7200
E-mail: aau@aaumail.org
Web site: http://www.aausports.org
This is a nonprofit organization devoted to the development of amateur sports. It publicizes events and provides support via local clubs.

American Management Association
1601 Broadway
New York, NY 10019
(877) 566-9441
Web site: http://www.amanet.org
The American Management Association is a nonprofit organization that enables individuals, companies, and organizations to search for management jobs, view training seminars and webcasts, and catch up on the latest reports in management.

AthletesCan: The Association of Canada's National Team
Athletes
1376 Bank Street, Suite 301
Ottawa, ON K1H 7Y3
Canada
(613) 526-4025
Web site: http://www.athletescan.com/main
This organization provides support, information, and
news about Canada's athletes.

Canadian Centre for Ethics in Sports
350-955 Green Valley Crescent
Ottawa, ON K2C 3Y4
Canada
(613) 521-3134
Web site: http://www.cces.ca/en/home
This center works on behalf of athletes, coaches, parents,
officials, and administrators to promote ethics in sport.

Club Managers Association of America
1733 King Street
Alexandria, VA 22314
(703) 739-9500
Web site: http://www.cmaa.org
This organization provides publications, educational resources, and career information for those interested in
managing golf courses.

International Special Events Society
401 North Michigan Avenue
Chicago, IL 60611-4267
(800) 688-4737
Web site: http://www.ises.com
The International Special Events Society provides event
    professionals with the latest news and a forum for
    community, and encourages the highest standards in
    business practices.

National Alliance for Youth Sports
National Headquarters
2050 Vista Parkway
West Palm Beach, FL 33411
(561) 684-1141
Web site: http://www.nays.org
This organization provides training and resources for volun-
    teer coaches and administrators involved in youth sports.

National Association of Collegiate Women Athletics
    Administrators (NACWAA)
2000 Baltimore Avenue
Kansas City, MO 64108
(816) 389-8200
Web site: http://www.nacwaa.org
This organization provides mentoring and support, a na-
    tional conference, and an online career center.

National Association of Girls and Women in Sport (NAGWS)
1900 Association Drive
Reston, VA 20191
(703) 476-3453
Web site: http://www.aahperd.org/nagws
This organization promotes participation of women in
  sports. It provides publications and internship and career information.

National Collegiate Athletic Association (NCAA)
700 West Washington Street
P.O. Box 6222
Indianapolis, IN 46206-6222
(317) 917-6222
Web site: http://www.ncaa.org
This organization organizes and regulates college sports.
  It provides news and other resources related to college
  athletics.

National Recreation and Park Association
22377 Belmont Ridge Road
Ashburn, VA 20148-4501
(800) 626-6772
Web site: http://www.nrpa.org
This group of citizen and professional organizations
  works to encourage the appreciation of outdoor

recreation and the parks and recreational facilities across the United States.

North American Society for Sport Management
NASSM Business Office
135 Winterwood Drive
Butler, PA 16001
(724) 482-6277
Web site: http://www.nassm.com
The North American Society for Sport Management champions professionals in sports, leisure, and recreation and promotes and encourages study, research, scholarly writing, and professional development in the area of sport management.

Right to Play International
Headquarters
65 Queen Street West
Thomson Building, Suite 1900
Toronto, ON M5H 2M5
Canada
(416) 498-1922

U.S. National Office:
Pam Peak
National Director

40 West 27th Street, Suite 930

New York, NY 10010

(646) 649-8280

Web site: http://www.righttoplay.com

This organization works with volunteers and partners to engage disadvantaged children in sports.

Sports Management Worldwide

1100 NW Glisan Street, Suite 2B

Portland, OR 97209

(877) SMWW-Now (769-9669)

Web site: http://www.smwwagency.com/sports/olympic_sports

This organization represents professional athletes in the Olympics.

WEB SITES

Due to the changing nature of Internet links, Rosen Publishing has developed an online list of Web sites related to the subject of this book. The site is updated regularly. Please use this link to access the list:

http://www.rosenlinks.com/gcsi/smgmt

FOR FURTHER READING

American Kinesiology Association. *Careers in Sports, Fitness, and Exercise*. Champaign, IL: Human Kinetics, 2010.

Bill, Karen. *Sport Management*. Exeter, UK: Learning Matters, 2009.

Devantier, Alecia T., and Carol A. Turkington. *Extraordinary Jobs in Sports*. New York, NY: Facts On File, Inc., 2006.

Favorito, Joseph. *Sport Management in Practice—Sport Publicity: A Practical Approach*. Burlington, MA: Butterworth-Heinemann, 2007.

Ferguson Publishing. *Discovering Careers for Your Future: Sports*. 2nd ed. New York, NY: Facts On File, Inc., 2005.

Ferguson Publishing. *Ferguson's Careers in Focus: Sports*. 4th ed. New York, NY: Ferguson Publishing Company, 2008.

Ferguson Publishing. *What Can I Do Now? Exploring Careers for Your Future*. 2nd ed. New York, NY: Ferguson Publishing Company, 2007.

Field, Shelly. *Career Opportunities in the Sports Industry*. New York, NY: Checkmark Books, 2010.

Field, Shelly. *Ferguson Career Coach: Managing Your Career in the Sports Industry*. New York, NY: Ferguson Publishing Company, 2008.

Finch, Jennie, and Ann Killion. *Throw Like a Girl: How to Dream Big and Believe in Yourself*. Chicago, IL: Triumph Books, 2011.

Fried, Gil. *Managing Sports Facilities*. Champaign, IL: Human Kinetics, 2009.

Greenwald, John. *Field Guides to Finding a New Career: Sports Industry*. New York, NY: Ferguson Publishing, 2010.

Heitzmann, Ray. *Careers for Sports Nuts & Other Athletic Types*. 3rd ed. Columbus, OH: McGraw-Hill, 2004.

Hopwood, Maria, James Skinner, and Paul Kitchin. *Sport Public Relations and Communication*. Burlington, MA: Elsevier, 2010.

Howell, Brian. *Sports* (Inside the Industry). San Francisco, CA: Essential Library, 2011.

Hunter, Nick. *Money in Sports* (Ethics of Sports). Chicago, IL: Heinemann Library, 2012.

Lindstrom, Erik, and Erika K. Arroyo. *Sports* (Discovering Careers). New York, NY: Facts On File, Inc., 2010.

Lussier, Robert, and David Kimball. *Applied Sport Management Skills*. Champaign, IL: Human Kinetics, 2009.

Masterman, Guy. *Strategic Sport Management, Olympic Edition*. Burlington, MA: Butterworth-Heinemann, 2009.

Materalexis, Lisa P., Carol A. Barr, and Mary A. Hums. *Principles and Practice of Sports Management*. 4th ed. Sudbury, MA: Jones & Bartlett Learning, 2012.

McLeish, Ewan. *Sports Industry* (A Closer Look: Global Industries). New York, NY: Rosen Publishing Group, Inc., 2011.

Pedersen, Paul, Janet Parks, Jerome Quarterman, and Lucie Thibault. *Contemporary Sports Management*. Champaign, IL: Human Kinetics, 2010.

Reeves, Diana Lindsey. *Career Ideas for Kids Who Like Sports*. New York, NY: Checkmark Books, 2007.

Schultz, Christian Dahl. *Ferguson Career Launcher: Professional Sports Organizations*. New York, NY: Ferguson Publishing Company, 2011.

Shropshire, Kenneth L., and Timothy Davis. *The Business of Sports Agents*. Philadelphia, PA: University of Pennsylvania Press, 2008.

Stotlar, David K. *Developing Successful Sport Marketing Plans*. Morgantown, WV: Fitness Information Technology, 2009.

Theodoraki, Eleni. *Olympic Event Management*. Burlington, MA: Butterworth-Heinemann, 2007.

Trenberth, Linda, and David Hassan, eds. *Managing Sport Business: An Introduction*. London, UK: Routledge, 2011.

Wells, Michelle, Andy Kreutzer, and Jim Kahler. *A Career in Sports: Advice from Sports Business Leaders*. Livonia, MI: M. Wells Enterprises, 2010.

Wong, Glenn M. *The Comprehensive Guide to Careers in Sports*. Sudbury, MA: Jones & Bartlett, 2008.

Youngman, Angela. *Sport and Active Leisure Industry*. Surrey, UK: Trotman, 2009.

BIBLIOGRAPHY

Amateur Athletic Union. "Event Sanctions." Retrieved July 16, 2011 (http://play.aausports.org/MembershipMenu/EventSanctions.aspx).

First Research. "Fitness Centers Industry Profile." Retrieved August 17, 2011 (http://www.firstresearch.com/industry-research/Fitness-Centers.html).

First Research. "Professional Sports Teams and Organization Industry Profile." Retrieved August 17, 2011 (http://www.firstresearch.com/industry-research/Professional-Sports-Teams-and-Organizations.html).

Georgetown University. "Master of Professional Studies in Sports Industry Management." Retrieved July 20, 2011 (http://scs.georgetown.edu/departments/14/master-of-professional-studies-in-sports-industry-management/about-the-program/curriculum).

Internet.com. "Ten Steps for Dealing with Other Cultures." Retrieved August 12, 2011 (http://www.projectmanagerplanet.com/leadership/article.php/3831671/10-Steps-for-Dealing-with-Different-Cultures.htm).

Lawyue, Matthew. "How to Choose a Sports Management Program." Bloomberg.com. Retrieved August 17, 2011 (http://www.businessweek.com/bschools/content/aug2008/bs20080818_920919.htm).

Lawyue, Matthew. "Students of Sports Management." *Bloomberg Businessweek*. Retrieved July 25, 2011 (http://images.businessweek.com/ss/08/08/0818_sports_management/index.htm).

Masteralexis, Lisa P., Carol A. Barr, and Mary A. Hums. *Principles and Practice of Sport Management.* 4th ed. Sudbury, MA: Jones & Bartlett Learning, 2012.

North American Society of Sport Management. "Sport Management Programs." Retrieved August 21, 2011 (http://www.nassm.com/InfoAbout/SportMgmtPrograms).

Parks, Janet B., Jerome Quarterman, and Lucie Thibault. *Contemporary Sport Management.* 3rd ed. Champaign, IL: Human Kinetics, 2007.

Philadelphia Eagles Media Guide. "Howie Roseman." Retrieved August 21, 2011 (http://legacy.philadelphiaeagles.com/eagles_files/html/ops_roseman_h_1.html).

Riddle, Joshua. "5 Things to Practice for Effective Communication." Workawesome.com. Retrieved August 17, 2011 (http://workawesome.com/communication/effective-communication-skills).

University of Arkansas. "Course Rotation Schedule: Recreation and Sports Management." Retrieved July 20, 2011 (http://recr.uark.edu/1174.php).

U.S. Bureau of Labor Statistics. *Occupational Handbook 2010–2011.* Retrieved July 18, 2011 (http://www.bls.gov/oco/ocos251.htm).

U.S. Sports Academy. "Introducing a Risk Management Model for Sports Venues." Sport Journal. Retrieved July 26, 2011 (http://www.thesportjournal.org/article/introducing-risk-assessment-model-sport-venues).

Womensportsjobs.com. "College Athletics." Retrieved July 24, 2011 (http://www.womensportsjobs.com/sportsjobs/jpcollege/jpcollege.htm).

INDEX

A

administrators, job duties of, 6–7
adventure travel management, 83–84
agencies, sports, 86–89
agents, sports, 19, 20, 24, 75–77
Amateur Athletic Union (AAU), 18
animals, sports involving, 10
athletics development managers, 42, 43
athletics directors, 15, 17, 40–42
   assistant/associate, 41–42

B

booking managers, 61
broadcast coordinators, 7
business/finance managers, 9, 11, 20, 42, 43, 57–58

C

Canadian Interuniversity Sports (CIS), 17

career plan, developing a, 68
coaches, 15, 17, 28
collective bargaining, 53
college sports, opportunities in, 16–17, 28, 39–50
   conference careers, 49–50
   managerial and administrative positions, 42–47
   senior management, 40–42
commissions, sports, 69–70
communications positions, 9, 12
   in college sports, 48–49
   in professional sports, 57
community relations managers, 48, 57
compliance managers, 47, 50
cruise line sports directors, 80

E

equipment managers, 43–45
ethics in sports, 74–75
event directors, 62
events management and administration, 6, 11, 12, 62–65, 85–97

finance and operations, 90–94
qualifications for, 96–97
risk management and security, 95–96
extreme sports, managing, 11–12

F

facilities managers, 12–13, 42, 43, 56, 60–65
managing crises, 63–64
responsibilities of, 61
fantasy sports camps, 29
finance, careers in, 71–73, 90–91
fitness directors, 80

G

game experience coordinators, 64
general managers, 6, 7–8, 20, 24, 52–53

H

high school/youth athletics, opportunities in, 14–16, 39
human resource manager and staff, 52, 53–54

I

information technology managers, 9, 20, 58–59
international events, participating in, 87
international level sports, 12, 20, 26, 87
internships, 35, 97

L

law, careers in, 73–75
leadership qualities, 46
league managers, 15
listening skills, need for, 24

M

managers
job duties, 6–7
as leaders, 46
media coordinators, 48, 49, 90
media relations, 6–7, 23, 48, 49, 57
mentoring, 55–56

N

National Collegiate Athletic Association (NCAA), 17, 28, 35, 66, 67
nonsports professionals in sports, 71–77

O

Olympics, 12, 13, 19, 85, 93, 94
operations managers, 61, 91–92
organizations, sports, 13, 66–70

P

player personnel, 52–54
professional outlook, developing a, 36–38
professional sports, opportunities in, 10, 19–20, 28, 51–59
described, 20
obtaining a job in, 59
player personnel, 52–54
professional sports organizations, 13
internships with, 35
managing, 66–70
participation in, 30–31
public relations/promotions, 9, 12, 20, 23, 48, 49, 50, 57, 61

R

recruiting managers, 45
registration managers, 93
Roseman, Howie, 7–8

S

scouts and scouting managers, 52, 53
security managers, 20, 64–65
semiprofessional sports, opportunities in, 17–19, 29
special events, management for, 13, 85–97
sport management and administration jobs
benefits of, 5, 12
competition for, 14, 20, 21, 28
described, 5, 6–20
education needed, 25–27, 32–36, 59
gaining practical experience, 27–30
outlook for, 28
preparing for, 21–31
skills needed for, 22–24
sports, participating in, 25–26
sports clubs, 82–83
sports industry, about the, 9–14, 36–37
sports management college degrees, 32–36
sports organizations/associations, managing, 13, 66–70
stadium managers and staff, 56

student athletic services manager, 47
summer programs and sports camps, 29

T

team managers, 15
ticket sales managers and staff, 20, 42, 43, 45–47, 57
tourism, sports, 78–80, 83–84
    dealing with people from different cultures, 82
tournament planners, 80

U

unions, player, 53

V

verbal communication skills, need for, 23–24
volunteering for teams and events, 27–30, 94, 97
volunteer management, 94

W

women's sports, 42

Y

youth athletics, opportunities in, 14–1

ABOUT THE AUTHOR

Jeri Freedman has a B.A. from Harvard University. She has written more than thirty young adult nonfiction books, including *Career Building Through Skinning and Modding, Careers in Emergency Medical Response Teams Search and Rescue, Careers in Computer Science and Programming, Women in the Workplace: Wages, Respect, and Equal Rights,* and *Professional Wrestling: Steroids In and Out of the Ring.*

PHOTO CREDITS

Cover, p. 1 © www.istockphoto.com/Stockphoto4u; pp. 4, 18, 40 © AP Images; p. 8 Drew Hallowell/Getty Images; p. 10 Matthew Stockman/Getty Images; pp. 15, 30 © Bill Aron/Photo Edit; p. 22 Wade Rackley/University of Tennessee Sports Information Department; p. 33 Jupiter, Brand X Pictures/Thinkstock; p. 37 © www.istockphoto.com/vm; p. 44 Brian Westerholt/Sports On Film; p. 48 Purdue University Athletics Communications; p. 52 Michael Zagaris/Getty Images; p. 54 Todd Rosenberg/Icon SMI; p. 55 © The Star Ledger/Mia Song/The Image Works; p. 58 © www.istockphoto.com/marcoroco; p. 62 Greensboro Coliseum Complex; pp. 65, 86 Courtesy of New York Road Runners; pp. 69, 95 Darren Carroll/Icon SMI; p. 70 Chris Trotman/Getty Images; p. 72 Mark Goldman/Icon SMI; p. 76 Alexander Tamargo/Getty Images; p. 79 © Carnival Cruise Lines; p. 81 Doral Golf Resort & Spa, a Marriot Resort; p. 83 KennStilger47/ Shutterstock.com; p. 88 Jonathan Daniel/Getty Images; p. 91 Valerio Pennicino/Getty Images; interior design elements: © www.istockphoto.com/hudiemm (grid pattern); http://lostandtaken.com (striped border); pp. 6, 21, 32, 39, 51, 60, 66, 71, 78, 85, 98, 110, 114, 118, 121, 127, 130, 132 (montage) © www.istockphoto.com, Shutterstock.com

Designer: Brian Garvey; Editor: Kathy Campbell;
Photo Researcher: Marty Levick